PICKLEBALL MINDSET

PICKLEBALL MINDSET

The Blueprint for
Peak Performance

Dayne Gingrich and Jill Martin

This publication is designed to provide accurate and authoritative information in regard to the subject matter covered. It is sold with the understanding that neither the authors nor the publisher are engaged in rendering legal, investment, accounting, medical, or other professional services. While the publisher and authors have used their best efforts in preparing this book, they make no representations or warranties with respect to the accuracy or completeness of the contents of this book and specifically disclaim any implied warranties of merchantability or fitness for a particular purpose. No warranty may be created or extended by sales representatives or written sales materials. The advice and strategies contained herein may not be suitable for your situation. You should consult with a professional when appropriate. Neither the publisher nor the authors shall be liable for any loss of profit or any other commercial damages, including but not limited to special, incidental, consequential, personal, or other damages.

This book is not intended as a substitute for the medical or psychological advice of healthcare or mental healthcare providers. Readers should consult a physician before starting exercise of any kind.

Some names and identifying details of people and events described in this book have been altered to protect their privacy.

First Paperback Edition April 2024

Paberback: 979-8-218-36982-8 | Ebook: 979-8-218-36983-5

Book design by Sarah Lahay
Cover Photograph by Jan Schmidtchen
Author Photograph by Polly and Ivan Pelly
Edited by Jenna Love-Schrader

www.coachdayne.com

For Liane, Logan, Andrew, Leif, and Finn,
the best cheerleaders we could hope for and the five
people who promised to buy our book before a word
was written.

Contents

ACKNOWLEDGMENTS

It took far more than a leap of faith to make this book a reality. It took heaps of them. This book is the product of hundreds of votes of confidence from family, friends, students, and mentors.

Most importantly, without much evidence that our idea for a book had legs, we received the unflagging support of our spouses, children, siblings, and parents. We didn't just ask for time to create the book. We asked for help! If you happened to be related to us by blood or marriage, you were called upon for advice, expertise, or a pep talk, and you each wholeheartedly delivered.

Like trying to improve our mental game, the writing and publishing process was harder and took longer than we anticipated. But our pickleball community's steadfast belief and support, on the court and online, kept us from even thinking of throwing in the towel.

There are too many friends to name who helped us along the way, and two deserve more appreciation than can be expressed on one page. Michael Challen and Lisa Smythe took on the daunting task of being our first reviewers. Their thoughtful feedback didn't just improve the book. It elevated our vision of what the book could be. A special thanks is also owed to David Peterson, who gently pushed us for many, *many* moons to stop editing and start publishing.

Then there are the strangers who lent their expertise to us for no other reason than their generous natures. Neither Tammy Leitner nor Liz Ruckdeschel knew us personally, yet both shared their invaluable wisdom about writing and helped us navigate the treacherous world of publishing.

Finally, to our partners and opponents, thank you for being part of the chest-pounding victories, the heart-wrenching defeats, the partnerships that imploded and the ones that felt divinely inspired, and the hours upon hours of drilling in between. The highs, lows, and even the tedium is what brought this book to life and continues to inspire us to become better players, partners, opponents, and people.

INTRODUCTION

Why We Wrote It and What's in It

DAYNE

IN MY HOUSE GROWING up, we didn't watch sports; we studied them. My dad and I logged more hours debating, dissecting, and analyzing NBA games than I could count. Even as an elementary school kid, my dad didn't quiz me on player stats or court strategy; he pushed me to consider the *internal* qualities that differentiated the good athletes from the great athletes. Why were Magic Johnson and Larry Bird better than their peers when neither were earth-shatteringly quick or particularly impressive jumpers? Their Hall of Fame greatness, my dad argued, couldn't be explained by their physical gifts alone; it was their ability to "concentrate under pressure" that separated them from more technically talented players.

Even though my dad challenged me to see *beyond* what we could see with our eyes in the best athletes from an early age, figuring out how to harness my internal potential did not come easily to me. From those early conversations, I had a lot more life to live, failures to survive, and athletes to coach before the seeds my dad planted took root, ultimately forming the basis of this book and shaping my career as a mental performance coach and professional pickleball player.

Getting from There to Here

From my earliest memories, I identified as a natural athlete and was good at any sport I picked up. As a teenager, I focused my efforts on tennis and basketball and had hoped to earn a college basketball scholarship. Though I experienced success on both courts in high school, my performance and achievements fell short of my abilities. Without the tools or maturity to manage my ego, fears, and doubts, I squandered opportunities, lost out on the chance to play college basketball, and ended up playing semi-professional tennis until injuries prematurely sidelined me. If you had asked me then what stood between me and reaching my potential, I would have pointed outward to all sorts of externalities—coaches, parents, teammates. Anywhere but inward. While I was naturally focused and thrived in the big moments, my underlying fear of failure and inability to tolerate not being the best handcuffed me. It would be many years until I could see past the pain of my disappointment and admit that what held me back was exactly what my father and I had been talking about since my earliest memories: weaknesses in my mental game.

After finishing my tournament tennis career in my mid-twenties, I began teaching tennis at a private club. I immediately gravitated toward the junior tennis scene, wanting to help young players maximize their potential. After a year of teaching the highest level of mechanics known at the time, I realized something was missing. My students struggled to execute in competition and weren't progressing at the rate I knew they could. I began to see that their technical skills weren't holding them back; their mindset was. I changed my entire teaching model. Instead of focusing the lion's share of our attention on technique and physical execution, I flipped the ratio and folded mechanical skills into the bigger picture of mental performance strategies. **The power of the mind was going to be the driver of their performance, not their racquet angle at contact.** The difference in my athletes' performance was immediate: The stress of trying to be mechanically perfect disappeared as if a huge weight had been lifted. Instead, they came to the court driven to find the emotional clarity that would allow them to perform to their fullest.

Soon after, word spread, and I became inundated with calls from parents who wanted me to help their kids. In the face of this new demand for coaching that prioritized the mental aspect of the game, I committed to learning more about what it meant to be a mentally dominant athlete. I read, listened, and watched every book, tape, and VHS on the topic (yes, I said *tape* and *VHS*). While studying helped me fill in gaps in my knowledge and gave me a broader perspective of what the field had to offer, where I learned the most was from the trenches. My own experiences as an athlete and those of the athletes I coached informed my philosophies more than what other coaches, sports psychologists, or athletes had to say on the topic.

Working with tennis players soon turned into basketball players, golfers, baseball players, football players, equestrian athletes, kids with test-taking anxiety, sales executives, and now pickleball players, both professional and amateur. Beginning in 2009, I started to share my coaching insights for peak mental performance on social media. By 2021, I had been writing about mental performance daily in a piecemeal fashion for over a decade. In the back of my mind, I was always planning on collecting my thoughts into a book, but life's daily concerns always seemed to jump the line and push the book to the back of the queue.

In late 2021, I met Jill, a yoga teacher and personal trainer, on the pickleball court when she joined a clinic one afternoon. She was the type of athlete I had rarely seen at the 4.0 level. Her ability to reach into the kitchen on one foot and never lose her balance blew my mind. After our first clinic, I quizzed her about how she was able to move the way she did and began to learn her approach to optimizing physical performance. I was struck by the similarities between our respective approaches to mindset and physical training and how complementary they were to one another. I had been struggling with the stress that pickleball was putting on my body and wanted to move with the same freedom and strength at the kitchen line as she did. She was struggling with mental performance issues and wanted to shake some mental habits that were holding her up on the court. Realizing we each had something to offer the other, we agreed to help each other; I would coach her and she would train me. It was during those sessions that this book started to migrate to the front of the line and make its way to the page.

JILL

When Dayne asked me to help him improve his strength and mobility for pickleball, I was in the middle of a desperately needed career transition. I had been practicing law for seventeen years, becoming increasingly dissatisfied in my chosen profession with each passing year. Though I had realized early on that practicing law was a dispositional mismatch that often left me depleted, many real and imagined factors kept me trudging along. A few years into practicing law, to balance out what felt like an increasingly unbalanced life, I started teaching a few yoga classes during my lunch breaks, which helped temporarily resuscitate my litigation-weary soul. As the years passed, the stark contrast in how each of my respective professions left me feeling made me question my decision to continue practicing law.

As life is apt to do, a cluster of events conspired to force a change. A dear friend died too young. A global pandemic emerged. Work became unbearably stressful. In such a short period, the world offered me ample evidence of what we all already know to be true: playing it safe isn't a guarantee, and life waits for no one. One day, bucking every cautious cell in my body, I pulled the ripcord and hung up my shingle, not entirely sure what the next chapter would look like.

It was during this crossroad that Dayne and I started training each other. Helping Dayne build confidence in his movement patterns was always the easy part of the bargain for me. Absorbing and applying Dayne's coaching was far more challenging. As Dayne pushed me to think differently about risks, fears, challenges, strengths, and vulnerabilities, my brain was often working on two problems simultaneously: how these strategies would play out on the court and what they meant for how I would navigate the next stage of my life *off the court*. I'd frequently leave our conversations with a plan for how to combat tournament nerves only to realize that I was really practicing skills to manage the jungle of unknowns that had grown when I left the

> **My brain was often working on two problems simultaneously: how these strategies would play out on the court and what they meant for how I would navigate the next stage of my life off the court.**

safety net of my law practice. The longer we trained together, the more I realized that my obsession with pickleball wasn't driven by a desire to master the *physical game*. Reaching a podium or becoming a 5.0 player was not my holy grail. Pickleball had become the playground on which I'd chosen to learn how to improve my human performance.

By my nature and profession, I have never been shy about asking questions when I don't understand something. The more I viewed pickleball as a way to work through mental habits that had held me up *on and off the court*, the more I pressed Dayne for a deeper understanding of his mental performance strategies. Often what seemed intuitive to him as a lifelong athlete was opaque and inaccessible to me. At some point after my seven millionth text message demanding clarification, I texted back, *We should write a book.*

DAYNE

When Jill suggested we write a book, I agreed to the idea, not knowing why I was agreeing other than something just "felt" right. What happened next cemented my decision: In *less than two weeks*, she had read *everything* I had written on social media since 2009. Soon, I found myself on the receiving end of what could feel like an endless cross-examination of everything I had ever written or said about mental performance strategies.

What began in my mind ten years ago as a book that would assemble all my coaching strategies instead evolved into a synthesis of the innumerable conversations Jill and I had as she worked on becoming mentally dominant on and off the court. More than a lecture by a coach to an athlete, this book is a yearlong conversation about how to grow and nourish a confident mindset throughout the turbulent journey that we all encounter as athletes and humans.

This book is a conversation about how to grow and nourish a confident mindset throughout the turbulent journey that we all encounter as athletes and humans.

Unlike many mental performance books, you won't get my biased perspective of how well my strategies work, neatly appointed with cherry-picked success stories of the athletes that I've coached. In each chapter, I'll explain the what, why, and how of implementing a mental performance strategy and delve into how I've seen it play out in my athletic and coaching career. Then you'll hear Jill's candid assessment of her experience working to incorporate each strategy into her game and life. She shares her real-time bumps, bruises, and celebrations as she works to elevate her mental game. Jill brings her litigator's skepticism to the process and isn't shy about pushing back, questioning the applicability and practicality of my suggestions, and generally putting me through my paces.

As you'll see, Jill and I don't always agree. Often times, however, our tumultuous process of finding a common ground helped me clarify my coaching strategies and helped Jill integrate them into her game. Our hope is that our honest account not only challenges you to elevate your game but also leaves you thirsty to keep pushing through the mental barriers that affect your performance.

What You'll Learn from This Book

This book isn't about *how to play* pickleball. It's about *how to think* on the court and *prepare your mind* to optimize your perfor- mance. If you're look- ing for technique tips, court strategies, or

> This book isn't about *how to play* pickleball. It's about *how to think* on the court.

drills to improve your physical performance, you won't find them here. **The objective of this book, counter-intuitively, is *not* to help you reach more podiums. Instead, it's to challenge you to hit the pause button on your results-oriented goals, look beyond the medals, and create a mentally stronger player who walks on the court with unwavering self-belief and confidence.**

Our goal isn't that you passively absorb and accept our ideas as the gospel on mental performance strategies. Rather, our work is done not if we convince you that everything we have to say is *the way*, but if we provoke questions about your process, make you wrestle with the strategies we introduce, and cause you to reconsider your current blueprint for success.

1

STOP CHASING
THE WIN

DAYNE

IN MY FIRST YEAR playing professional pickleball, I was singularly focused on winning gold in both men's and mixed doubles at the 2021 Margaritaville USA Pickleball National Championships in Indian Wells, California. At the time, Nationals represented the most prestigious gold in the game. Winning the double gold would be the ultimate feather in my cap, solidifying my place at the senior pro table. Every day leading up to Nationals that year, I envisioned it, talked about it, and practiced for it.

My entire season was centered around chasing the biggest win. The timing was ideal: as the last tournament on the calendar, closing out with two golds would be the perfect exclamation point on the end of my first year on the professional pickleball circuit.

After battling it out with in an intense three-game match in the men's final with Dave Weinbach and a fifteen-point tie break game in the mixed final with Jennifer Dawson, we took gold in both brackets. Immediately following my last match, I was overcome with emotion. In that moment on the court, I couldn't have felt happier.

Then, something unexpected happened. As I went through my post-match stretching routine in my hotel that night, an overwhelming feeling of emptiness came over me. As the adrenaline that had taken me through the finals receded, the happiness I felt on the court was fading . . . and fast. Rather than relishing my victory, I felt confused and was left wondering, *Why don't I feel as incredible as I imagined I would having achieved my season-ending goals?*

After a few days of soul-searching, a mentor gently reminded me that I had the blueprint backward. I had anchored my focus on the gold rather than the *pursuit* of the gold and *the person I wanted to be* when I reached the podium. The podium had become my North Star rather than the process. For as many times as I had learned the lesson before, I was again reminded that the only meaningful goals are the internal ones. If we don't crave the pursuit and connect our process to who we want to become more than the win, we have zero chance of regularly finding the wins. Nationals affirmed that the only goal I should ever chase is out-working myself and anyone standing in my way. Every single day. That's it.

I am not saying I don't care about the win. I'm as competitive as anyone on the planet. What I've learned through both coaching and my own journey is that fiercely wanting the win isn't enough to power sustained athletic success. Result-driven goals invariably falter in the face of setbacks and injuries and can become self-defeating when left to operate unchecked by a higher purpose. **To attain peak mental and physical performance, we need to connect to the *internal purpose* that lies beneath the *external goal*.** This chapter explores how to tap into our most sustainable fuel source rooted in *who we want to become on the journey* rather than *where we want to end up*.

Why Purpose Matters

As a mental performance coach, athletes most often come to me when they are experiencing a disconnect between their abilities and their performance. Bluntly speaking, athletes don't typically search me out when they are regularly making their way to the top of the podium. Instead, something is standing between what they know they can do and their ability to execute, which manifests in disappointing performance out-comes. Ultimately, most of the athletes I coach are seeking to develop the mental and emotional skills required to optimize their performance and get better at doing their job of coming out on top.

Since a competitive athlete's primary objective is to win, it begs the question: Why would I, as a coach whose job it is to help athletes achieve their goals, sug-gest making winning second fiddle to anything else? After over thirty years of coaching, I can tell you with certainty that the power of the win to drive motivation falters when athletes struggle and experience normal ebbs in their performance. *All* athletes experience highs, lows, and spirit-testing struggles no matter how talented they are. The ones with staying power have figured out a way to persevere during the droughts, knowing that the rain always comes again. In the dry periods when the losses are racking up faster than the wins, what keeps an athlete competing if the win is the only focal point on the horizon? What is the impetus to drill one more hour when last week's drilling didn't yield the intended dividends?

I've heard from more athletes than I can remember who believe that they will work harder, want it more, and won't quit even when it gets soul-crushingly difficult. They believe it, and I want to believe them, but the numbers tell a different story. What's the differentiator between those who prevail and those who walk away? The athletes who connect their extrinsic goals to an intrinsic vision of who they want to become are unstoppable. Nothing is too tiring, frustrating, or out of reach for those who allow the wins, rankings, and medals to be a byproduct of their pursuit of a deeper purpose.

> **Nothing is too tiring, frustrating, or out of reach for those who allow the wins, rankings, and medals to be a byproduct of their pursuit of a deeper purpose.**

Finding My Purpose

My two-act athletic career, separated by almost thirty years, is about as close as you'll get to a case study on the power of purpose. As a young athlete, I had all the attributes needed to reach the highest levels of success in tennis. I had a natural gift, was intensely focused, had parents who fostered my athletic gifts, and lived to compete. Yet relative to my potential, I underperformed on the semiprofessional tennis circuit.

Fast-forward a few decades and I've experienced more success in the few years that I've played professional pickleball than I ever did in tennis. My body is older, my life is busier with a family and career, and my hours on the pickleball court don't come close to touching the amount of time I spent with a tennis racquet in my hand. What changed? My mindset and purpose. Of course, my mindset has evolved and changed over a lifetime—whose hasn't? I've also benefited from years of studying and coaching mental performance strategies, but the fundamental shift is my motivation.

As a young athlete, I was the epitome of a results-driven performer. The myopic lens of my ego dictated my practice, performance, and mindset; my singular purpose on the court was to beat everyone and be the best. My power source—that relentless desire to win— was also my poison. The strength of my goals, however, was not a match for the underbelly of my ego—my fear of not being good enough. My paralyzing fear of failure, like a metastasizing cancer, invaded each of the decisions I made, ultimately undermining my ability to perform to my potential. Losses ended with breaking racquets and coming far too close to jumping the net to fight those who had bested me. Driven solely by the desire to win, losses were so painful that it was easier to bow out of opportunities when I couldn't ensure that I'd come out on top. My professional tennis career was one of my ego's first casualties.

Off the tennis court, my fears continued to dog me for years, subtly but persistently running interference with my ability to fully commit and invest myself in my life and my business. After a decade of coaching tennis, I began to notice the invisible thread that ran through my athletes who were achieving at the highest levels. I observed time and again that the athletes with a deeper drive seemed to have access to an extra oxygen tank that kicked in at the highest altitudes, while those driven by the win gasped for air. Excavating for the deeper purpose with all my athletes became an invaluable tool in my coaching arsenal, providing access to higher levels of resilience, grit, and determination.

As a rule, I won't preach to my athletes what I'm not willing to practice myself. That meant it was finally time to face the demons that had plagued my athletic career and continued to muddy my decision-making. Forced to finally pull the curtain back instead of blaming everyone else for my shortcomings, I looked at the patterns of fear and doubt that short-circuited the connection between my abilities and my performance. It was at that moment that my purpose became to stop letting fear drive my decisions and actions.

In my mid-thirties by that point, I had just stepped away from the security of teaching tennis and dove into the uncharted territory of launching my career as a mental performance coach. As a new entrepreneur, I started off driven solely by attaining financial success, just as I had blindly chased the win as an athlete. When I finally was able to tap into a deeper purpose, I turned the spotlight from the pursuit of monetary success to the intentional mission of living free from the self-imposed prison of my fears. Once I made the mental shift, it was as if a black light had been cast over my personal history, revealing all the decisions, actions, and outcomes that had been infected by my fears. To my horror, there were body bags hiding behind every corner.

Despite how revelatory a realization it was, unwinding an entrenched way of thinking doesn't happen overnight. It was gut-wrenching work, but the mere awareness of the chokehold that fear had held over me made it a visible player at the table. Once I could see it, I could decide how much voting power to give it.

When my daughter was born a few years later, my commitment solidified into an unyielding determination to model a mindset for her anchored in self-belief rather than self-sabotaging doubt. Rooting my path to the person I wanted to become—the father I wanted to be—rather than to the transitory personal glory of a

> **Rooting my path to the person I wanted to become allowed me to access a bottomless well of resolve.**

win, allowed me to access a bottomless well of resolve.

With more than a decade of conscious practice, my fears have quieted, their shouts softening to whispers—still present but far less potent. My daughter has become an increasingly independent teenager with her own aspirations, struggles, and accomplishments. She needs me in less obvious ways now, which occasionally fools me into thinking she doesn't need me anymore, but my wife reminds me that she is always watching, listening, taking in how we show up in our lives, wrestle with our demons, and overcome our obstacles. This knowledge, and the commitment I made when she was born, help silence the fears when they threaten to wrest back the role of decision-maker. Every day that I train, that I put myself on the line in tournaments, that I watch an extra hour of film, I do it so that she knows with the same certainty that the sun rises in the morning and sets at night, that whatever she sees for herself is possible with the right mindset.

By the time I picked up a pickleball paddle when I was close to fifty, my mind had well-worn grooves that helped to keep my vision tied to the macro of who I want to be rather than the micro of where I want to go. Nevertheless, it's easy for my ego to gain traction when sponsorship and prize money are at stake, threatening to obscure my view of the big picture. Tangible, short-term rewards continue to tempt me and demand that

I engage in a daily, conscious practice of remaining true to my inner purpose, trusting that the external outcomes will follow. When the siren song of the win calls, I gently remind myself that no mindset shift has been more fulfilling and worthy of every ounce of pain, frustration, and work than connecting my path to my deeper purpose.

Finding Your Purpose

Identifying an extrinsic goal, such as, "I want to become a 5.0 pickleball player," is easy for most athletes. Figuring out the internal driver is the tricky part. Steeped in a culture biased toward bragging rights with little attention placed on the "why" behind pursuit of the "what," most of us don't have a lot of practice at identifying the deeper purpose behind the work we do. It makes sense. We have bills to pay and families to raise, which can make contemplation of a deeper purpose feel like a luxury outside of our budget. **Goals and purpose are *not* mutually exclusive. Rather, the sweet spot is the *intersection of goal and purpose*; we**

don't have to throw out the former to connect it to the latter.

Think of your goal as a starting point. Assume for the moment your goal is to become a 5.0 pickleball player. Now replace the idea of a *goal* with a *vision*. Paint a detailed picture of what the process of becoming a 5.0 player will look like. What parts of you will be stretched in the process? How would attaining your vision affect others in your life? Why is that vision meaningful to you, and why did you choose it?

If you keep coming back to more "goal-oriented" answers, keep pressing. Every time you think you've mined your deepest purpose, dig one layer deeper until you reach your bedrock. Then, cultivate a detailed emotional connection to the vision of the person you've committed to becoming. That connection will be your lifeline to staying focused and motivated when it feels impossible to keep going. Most athletes stop not because of a lack of talent or good coaching, but because they didn't have a powerful enough connection to their why.

How to Find Your Purpose

STEP 1: Identify your GOALS

- Why did you choose those goals?
- Why are they meaningful to you?

STEP 2: Replace your goals with a VISION of the person you need to be to achieve those goals.

- How does that player train?
- What does she look like when she steps on the court?

STEP 3: Create EMOTIONAL CONNECTION to your vision.

- What does that player feel like on and off the court?
- What does her intesity, focus, passion, and grit feel like?

Everyone's inner drivers are unique to their life experience and goals. I spent the first half of my coaching career primarily working with younger athletes who, by the very fact of their age, are still developing their sense of self and their vision of who they want to be. Pickleball created the unique opportunity to coach adult athletes, who have a clearer sense of not only who they currently are, but how they want to show up in their second or third act. They've experienced enough successes and failures to know what's worked for them, what's gotten in their way, and what they want to do differently. When there is less sand left in the hourglass, a strong internal purpose can have unstoppable power.

The journey of one of the amateur pickleball players I coach, Shannon, provides a weekly reminder of the potency of connecting goals with a core purpose. I originally met Shannon on the tennis court as she was coming up for air after having survived getting four small children through diapers. With no racquet sport background, Shannon was persuaded by a fellow mom to give the sport a try. To say that Shannon got hooked would be an understatement. She put her formidable force and energy behind becoming the best tennis player she could be.

Beneath Shannon's easy smile resides a beast with an unparalleled competitive drive. She runs at such a high frequency that sometimes I think she might be vibrating. What I love about Shannon is that she is unapologetic about the fact that she comes to the court to win, every time. She'll be the first to tell you that she'd rather cough up blood than throw in the towel.

It would be a mistake, however, to assume that her competitive drive is what launched her to unprecedented levels of success on the tennis court as a middle-aged woman. Not to throw shade on pickleball, but do you know how much harder it is to become good at tennis without a racquet background? Within two years of starting tennis, Shannon was competing against and beating former collegiate tennis players who had started swinging a racquet just after learning to walk.

If you talk to Shannon long enough, you'll learn that there is something far more important to her than the win. Okay, that's probably hyperbole with Mrs. I'll-Sacrifice-an-Organ-Before-I-Lose, but let's just say *equally* important as the win. As a child, Shannon had big dreams and visions of being a Supreme Court justice or a famous civil rights lawyer. She grew up enlivened by the idea of how she'd change the world. (And she *has changed* the world, but in a different way than she had imagined.) She tabled her career aspirations and dedicated herself to raising her children, but it left her wondering, *What could I have accomplished if I had taken a different path?*

It was scratching that itch, answering that curiosity—What am I capable of when I throw all my weight behind a goal?—that pushed Shannon to attain the improbable. It made her take notes after every lesson. It made her write down post-game observations about every opponent. It made her keep practicing when she'd been up all night with sick kids. It allowed her to shrug off the judgments of those who couldn't understand why she was treating her recreational tennis career like she was preparing to argue in front of the Supreme Court. She *was* arguing her most important case; it's just that she was her own judge and jury. That drive to prove herself carried her through the bitter defeats, the self-doubt, and judgments with a far more steadfast engine than the desire to win ever could have.

The smart woman she is, she eventually left behind that oversized racquet and court and is continuing to dominate on the pickleball court. If you find yourself across the net from her at a tournament, the best advice I can give you is, *You'd better bring your A-game because that's the only game she plays.*

Does every successful athlete have to connect to a deeper purpose? Nah, I am sure that some athletes can be propelled by the win alone. What's the downside of investing in yourself rather than setting your sights on bragging rights alone? No one can guarantee that you'll make it to the top of the podium, but it will be far more gratifying if you like the person you've become when you get there.

JILL

Legend has it that the first time Dayne played pickleball, he played so intensely for so many hours that he burned out his quads and couldn't walk for days. When he made his way back on the court, it didn't take long for him to know that he'd soon be playing pickleball professionally. There was no "playing just for fun" chapter in his pickleball career. From the outset, he knew that pickleball would provide the opportunity to connect his mental performance training, competitive drive, and vision of the person he had committed to becoming since leaving the tennis court.

My story starts and ends a bit differently. First off, my quads are *way* stronger than Dayne's, so there is *no version* of my story that ends with gassed muscles. Beyond our incomparable endurance, our motivation on the court also parts ways. Unlike Dayne's unwavering internally focused drive, my reasons for playing evolved over time:

Act I: Survival

Six months before COVID-19 shut down the world, a friend asked me to join her in a biweekly "Introduction to Pickleball" clinic. The clinic was smack in the middle of the workday. At the time, my life resembled that of an overly ambitious plate juggler who knew that at any moment porcelain was going to start flying. Between my professional and parenting obligations, my time and attention were already spread as thin as old parchment, threatening to rip if even one more carpool obligation was thrown in the mix. I had never heard of pickleball, and the notion of dedicating precious hours to learn to hit a wiffle ball with an oversize ping-pong paddle struck me as absurd. I politely declined.

Like the rest of the world, in March 2020, the breakneck pace at which I had been living grinded to a halt. The civil court system had all but closed, slowing down my legal work to a trickle. My taxi services for my sons had dried up as Zoom took the place of brick-and-mortar schools and athletic fields. When my friend proposed the same pickleball clinic again that spring, it seemed like a perfectly reasonable way to escape from pickling vegetables, knitting baby hats, and the other host of odd hobbies I had picked up from the confines of my home.

By the end of my first lesson, I was hooked in that unexplainable way that only pickleball seems to engender. On my drive home, I called my running buddy, Jules, and directed her to put down her burgeoning, pandemic-borne sourdough starter and sign up for the clinic. This is a woman with whom I had previously run up mountains and competed in triathlons, so proposing a sport known for its silver-haired aficionados could have been a tough sell. There is nothing like spending months locked in a house with your family to open your mind to new possibilities! Luckily, it was love at first dink for Jules too.

In that first year on the court, pickleball provided the most glorious reprieve from the dystopian reality of our pandemic-era lives. The only motivation needed to get me to the courts was the knowledge that I got to chase a ball seven feet apart from people I didn't birth or marry. Jules and I played a ridiculous amount because: (1) With our personal and professional obligations still on hold due to mutating spike proteins, we could; and (2) We couldn't stop.

Act II: Competition

As lifelong athletes, Jules and I were destined to be only passing visitors in the just-for-fun pickle-ball way station. By equal parts luck and design, we grew a pickleball community of like-minded women, who put their ample athleticism and energy into improving their game. We sweated through clinics together, drilled our drops, and high-fived one another as we body-bagged each other.

Eventually, we ventured outside the sanctuary of our friendly round robins and into the Wild West of tournament play. As our play became more competitive, my drive shifted into a new gear that was no stranger to me. For good and bad, I'm not a dabbler. Once I set my sights on a target, my desire to gain mastery can be unrelenting. I've been to the Type A++ rodeo enough times to see the upsides and downsides of my intensity. Left unabated, my goal-driven nature either propels me forward at enviable speed or leaves me in a puddle.

My hyperfocus has come in handy plenty of times. It powered me through law school, the bar exam, and mind-numbing document reviews, but it can also bleed into deafening perfectionism— my greatest asset *and* liability. Naturally prone to perfectionistic tendencies, practicing law for almost two decades had amplified my exacting inclinations. Civil litigation had exposed me to a disproportionate sample size of human errors that resulted in catastrophic consequences. In the real world, most missteps don't lead to disaster, but harmless blunders simply don't make their way to an attorney's desk. Additionally, like any competent attorney, I was meticulous in my work to ensure that I would never harm a client through an oversight. Waking up in a cold sweat over an imagined error or omission was a monthly occurrence. Unknowingly, I had spent years as an attorney feeding my inner perfectionist, who started to creep its way into all aspects of my life, including the pickleball court.

Once my intensity attached itself to my pickleball paddle, my progression as a player mirrored the trend lines of a wartime stock market. The ups and downs were fast, furious, and completely unpredictable. One day, I'd play like I was born with a paddle in my hand; the next, it was as if I had never hit a pickleball before. Having good days and bad days on the court certainly isn't unique to me, but my swings seemed more dramatic. Minimally, my *tolerance* for my variability was woefully low.

During this period, my goals on the court were narrow and strangely specific. Whereas many of my fellow pickleball fanatics aimed to become a 5.0 player, my sights barely reached past my own paddle. Instead of imagining myself on the top of a podium, my drive was toward mastery of shots, almost as if detached from playing against people in an actual game. Winning wasn't so much of the goal, though I quite like to win! Losing was tolerable, but falling short of my self-imposed expectations of how I should be able to perform was not. In hindsight, my quest to master certain shots came from the desire to insulate myself from the discomfort of making errors while playing—as if any amount of drilling could guarantee perfection. While drilling a shot to execute it with greater consistency is worthwhile, it doesn't take a mental performance coach to know that attempting to eliminate errors instead of learning to manage them is a fool's errand.

Tens of thousands of balls and several tournaments later, I realized my advancement wasn't being slowed down by my seeming inability to master certain shots. It was hamstrung by something immune to my drilling: my mental game. I started taking inventory of the circumstances that lampooned me. Three patterns stood out: First, if I started off a day on the court with more than a few unforced errors, my confidence would get shaken, my body tightened, and my game would irretrievably nosedive. One error seemed to beget the next despite the various strategies I tried to extract myself from my self-perpetuating error spiral. Second, I was blind to my own contributions and strengths. Dayne encourages his students to lean into their superpowers rather than giving undo focus to shoring up weaknesses. While I could write a dissertation on the weaknesses in my game, I had little clarity on my strengths. Third, even in the low stakes arena of pickleball, I found myself shying away from taking on games, opponents, and partners that felt too far outside my comfort zone.

A perfectly reasonable response to these observations would be to return to my pickleball roots—treating the game as a fun hobby and distraction, rather than my own personal Olympics. After all, this is pickleball, not a global peace treaty. But I wasn't ready to throw in the towel, and I was tired of letting my own standards sabotage me.

Picking up a pickleball paddle had coincided with a time in my life when I had come to the unsettling realization that I had let too much time pass avoiding what made me uncomfortable and shying away from risks. I had stayed in a safe career for seventeen years that paid the bills, but often wondered what life could be like if I could find the courage to shutter my legal practice and open the door to a new professional chapter.

The pickleball court would become my practice lab for building resilience to errors, taking risks, and seeing and owning my strengths.

My cautious and perfectionistic nature wasn't going to be reversed overnight. I needed a small, bubble-wrapped playground on which to practice. The pickleball court would become my practice lab for building resilience to errors, taking risks, and seeing and owning my strengths. It was time, once again, to switch gears and shift my focus.

Act III: The Deep Dive

I mentally shredded the list of shots I had wanted to master and jotted down a new list:

> Pickleball Goals
> 1. Improve my tolerance for errors.
> 2. Recognize my own strengths.
> 3. Take more risks.

This short list should be easy to accomplish, no?

Given the amount of time I found myself slinking off to the court, I was guaranteed high reps for building my emotional resilience muscles. The stakes were perfectly low: It was far less risky to develop a tolerance for error on a pickleball court than in a courtroom. Stepping outside my comfort zone on the pickleball courts was child's play compared to shaking things up in my professional endeavors.

You could argue that being okay with popping up your drop is so far afield from accepting your fallibility in higher-stakes circumstances that one could never prepare you for the other. I like to think of it as the most fun version of exposure therapy. Throwing someone with a shark phobia into a shark tank in chummed waters probably wouldn't yield optimal results. Pickleball is just my version of watching Shark Week before dipping my toe in the ocean.

Besides, with pickleball, I could count on making tens, hundreds, thousands of mistakes a week. It gave me more practice in a shorter time window to build resilience to errors than anything I could imagine. And there was a bonus: no one would die or sue me if I made a mistake.

I also had the right coach for the job. On social media and on the court, Dayne appears serious, tough, and more ready to snarl "Let's goooooo!" than to hand out gold stars or give a pat on the back. But as a coach, he's a surprising combination of hard-assed and soft-hearted. If you're willing to put the work in, he will dive deep, patiently listen to what scares you, and create an action plan to help you reach your goals. He's even willing to see and believe in your superpowers when you can't see and believe in them yet. When I told him pickleball wasn't just about pickleball for me, that it was about all the life skills I wanted to learn on the court, he didn't miss a beat. He was on board and has been my biggest cheerleader ever since.

Shifting my focus from *attaining perfection* to *managing my imperfection* both on and off the court didn't change my game or me overnight. Once I started to make the shift, I could *sometimes* see my misses and mishits for what they were: opportunities to practice letting myself be human. I used to worry that I'd lose my drive if I eased up on myself. Instead, the opposite has happened; it's as if each time I allow for the possibility of errors, I create more bandwidth to take bigger risks with more confidence, focus, and energy. More importantly, learning to release myself from the confines of my exacting standards motivates me at a cellular level in a way that reaching the podium as a 5.0 never could.

There is a temptation to write a chronically forward-progressing narrative in which I effortlessly implement Dayne's strategies and become mentally bulletproof. It's not honest, realistic, or helpful though. Uncoiling the hose of lifelong mental habits has been slow-going. When I was twenty-one, I housesat for a couple who was then the age I am now. Every kitchen cabinet I opened housed a sticky note with a positive affirmation. What I quietly scoffed at then, I understand now. It's painstaking work to change long-held ways of interacting with the world. Without daily conscious practice, my commitment to building resilience to imperfection slips through my fingers like the finest-grain sand. Who knows what the inside of my cabinets will look like by the time I'm a 5.0 player?

As I worked my way through Dayne's mental performance strategies, it frequently felt as if I were taking two steps forward and one step back, with my inner-perfectionist rearing her head at the most inconvenient times, sometimes threatening to stage an outright coup. Luckily, my coach and partners are the best perfectionist-hostage-negotiating SWAT team in the game and are at the ready to remind me when my inner critic's mouth needs a fresh duct-taping. While I can't tell you that focusing on who I am becoming has been easy or even instantly rewarding, I can tell you that there is no more fun place to work on the hard stuff than the pickleball court.

2

PRE-ACCEPT WHAT YOU CAN'T CONTROL

DAYNE

THE CROWD HAS FINALLY had enough and is becoming restless. I start to hear boos from the spectators behind me. They simply want the match to resume, as do I. Circumstances beyond my control have caused our match to grind to a halt, threatening to slowly kill our confidence and give hope to our opponents.

It was the third game of a live-streamed match on center court. My partner believed the referee made a bad call against him and got mentally trapped in contesting the call. Instead of lodging his complaint and moving on to the next point, he argued with the referee for over ten minutes as our momentum slowly drained from the court. I had a choice to make in that moment: I could join him in his anger; grab him by the back of the shirt, and beg him to start the next point; or I could take total control of my own mental and emotional game. Knowing the first two options were out of my control, I chose door number three. I walked to the baseline, turned my back to the increasingly hostile exchange between my partner and the referee, and stared blankly at the back fence.

Instead of going down the rabbit hole with my partner, I intentionally took control of my own internal game. As I stared at the fence, I concentrated on slowing down my breathing while visualizing how I wanted to play when the match resumed. Within thirty seconds of beginning my mental reset routine, his angry voice disappeared, leaving me at peace within my own personal process. "Players, resume play" was the next thing I heard. I took a final breath, turned back around, and was ready to drop back into the match where we left off.

In a tournament or even a rec game, we lack control over an infinite number of variables: weather, line calls, our opponents' performance, our partner's performance, makes, misses, injuries, illness, and on and on and on. The biggest "uncontrollable" is the one that matters most: the outcome of the match. In the face of so much uncertainty, our minds often engage in a misguided attempt to control the variables outside our reach and force the result we want. The tighter we grasp to the desired outcome, the farther away it seems to drift from us.

That day on the court, as my partner argued his case, the temptation was so great to try to force my partner to drop the argument and stay with me, locked into the next point. If I had let my focus become attached to the outcome of the match, I would have become consumed by the knowledge that every moment he continued to argue, we'd be pulled further from a win. My partner's reactions and decisions were so far outside my control that my only choice was to remain committed to preserving my own focus so that I was ready to make the next set of decisions and reactions that came my way.

In pickleball, we have control over four variables at most:

1. Our pre-acceptance of all possible outcomes before we step on the court
2. Our pregame preparation
3. Our on-court decisions
4. Our on-court reactions

Our pre-acceptance of all possible outcomes and preparation prime our mental canvas for our on-court reactions and decisions. In other words, **the more confidence we have in our preparation and ability to respond to anything that comes our way, the better we make successful course corrections to the rapidly changing circumstances on the court.** This chapter explores how to successfully build resilience to all the variables outside of our control and walk the tightrope of pre-accepting the possibility of any and all outcomes while still fighting like hell for the one we want.

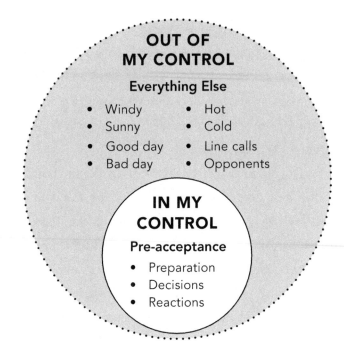

Pre-Acceptance

We've all found ourselves in a game where not even fifteen minutes have elapsed since the first serve, and somehow our opponents have steamrolled their way to a point or two from eleven. Pickleball games can play out so quickly with such volatile momentum swings that it is essential to develop strategies to manage our emotional and mental response to the variables we can't control and maximize our influence over the ones we can. Otherwise, during a downward momentum swing, we risk getting locked into a counterproductive thought process and letting the game get away from us before we can adjust and pivot.

During these runs, when it feels like the bottom is dropping out of our game plan, our mind often intuitively gets locked in on the win or the loss and tries to wrest control of that which seems to be pulling us further away from the win: We get agitated by the sun blinding us while we run down lobs. Not only does the sun not care, but our opponents lob us more. We double down on not missing and find that we only miss more. We silently will our partner to start making his shots; instead, his ball keeps finding the wrong side of the tape. The more we try to control the uncontrollable, the tighter and more anxious we become, diminishing our ability to

The more we try to control the uncontrollable, the tighter and more anxious we become, diminishing our ability to adjust, manage, and respond to the experience in real time.

adjust, manage, and respond to the experience in real time. In that state of tension, we actually *lose* control of the ability to draw on the very few elements within our control: our decisions and reactions.

The key to optimizing our performance under tension is maximizing our training of what we *do* control and *pre-accepting that all outcomes, good or bad, are possible*, which opens the door to a strong, clear state of mind for the next decision. What is pre-acceptance? **It's the intentional acceptance of and mental preparation for all the factors outside our control that will influence the outcome of our match**. It's *pre*-acceptance because it is a purposeful practice and exercise that happens *before* stepping on the court, like a dynamic warm-up for our mind.

The notion of accepting the uncontrollable nature of everything around us isn't novel. It's the crux of world religions, meditation practices, recovery modalities, and many other belief systems designed to help our minds cope with the constant uncertainty that surrounds us. The sports-specific practice of pre-acceptance imports these well-honed strategies into our quiver of mental performance tools. I originally was introduced to the concept of pre-acceptance in athletics when I was competing in golf at an amateur level. To my intense irritation, it became clear that perfect execution of a golf swing simply didn't dictate the outcome. I had to learn to pre-accept that, even if I made the perfect swing, the ball could get caught by a gust of wind, derailed by a sprinkler head, or even carried away by a squirrel (true story!). In pickleball, pre-acceptance has continued to provide me with a trainable tool to manage my strong desire to dictate an outcome that exists far beyond the reach of my control.

Pre-Acceptance Versus Pre-Expecting

Before we inadvertently give our minds permission to imagine a fantasized future of negative externalities and outcomes, let's get clear on the difference between *accepting* and *expecting*. *Pre-acceptance* is not *expecting* and preparing for a negative outcome. *Expecting* and preparing for a negative outcome is tantamount to engaging in a purposeful anxiety practice and anticipating, visualizing, or planning for the worst. The very last way we want to use the power of our mind is to envision and become fearful of an outcome we don't want. Most athletes instinctively go to the negative already, and we want to train ourselves *away from* that inclination, *not toward it.* Think of acceptance versus expectation like a meditative breath: When we *accept*, we exhale and release control. When we *expect*, we hold our breath and clench our fists tighter around control.

On the other end of the spectrum, pre-*expecting* can take the similarly unhelpful form of anticipating or planning for the best. In chapter 3, we'll explore the benefit of visualizing perfect shots, games, and matches beyond even our present execution abilities. **The important bedfellow to visualization, however, is detachment from our on-court results. When we *expect* a good result and things don't go according to plan, we can't adjust to and manage the experience in real time.** We get blamey and "complainy." We point fingers at our partners, line calls, the weather, and the referee, but most damningly, we lose our ability to pivot in the face of the unexpected. The challenge becomes visualizing perfect execution *and* pre-accepting the full range of possibilities.

If we can train ourselves before we step onto the court to accept the possibility of any outcomes, we can release the control tension valve and laser in on the ultimate objective: mental dominance in response to anything that might happen. Every decision and reaction becomes underpinned by the knowledge that we are prepared for anything that happens and are therefore mentally unbreakable. If I have pre-accepted that the

> **We can release the control tension valve and laser in on the ultimate objective: mental dominance in response to anything that might happen.**

sun might be in my eyes, the wind might be against me, my partner might implode, my opponent might have the best day of his life, then I can meet every possibility with complete mental confidence. I might not win. I might even have the worst game of my life. But I will not break. In this state, I'll have the best shot of effectively responding to whatever comes at me.

How to Practice Pre-Acceptance

Pre-acceptance is a *trained* skill, no different than any other skill on the court. It takes time, repetition, intentionality, and discipline. As with all mental performance training, it can feel tougher than physical training with less instantaneous results. It's much easier to grind your dink than prepare to stay present and agile in the face of the chaos.

The nuts and bolts of a pre-acceptance practice will be as individual as the player. The key is finding the method of practice that works best for you and identifying the right questions to ask yourself. First, figure out the method of self-talk that is most comfortable for you. It might take the shape of writing, talking out loud to yourself, recording yourself, or just imagining. Once you settle on the *how*, tackle the *what*. Ask yourself, "What does pre-acceptance mean to me at my current skill level with my unique set of challenges and strengths today?" Start simple. Maybe it's as basic as, "I'll accept that it might be hotter during my tournament than during rec play, and I may get more easily fatigued." "I'll accept that the wind may frustrate me." As you grow your pre-acceptance muscles, begin to up the ante and progressively add more variables and complexity, staying within a manageable zone that doesn't throw you off the deep end. Then, repeat, repeat, and repeat again, letting the practice organically grow from there.

1. CHOOSE METHOD OF PRACTICE

Pick a method of self-talk:

- writing
- recording yourself
- imaging
- talking out loud to yourself

2. DEFINE PRE-ACCEPTANCE

Ask yourself: What does pre-acceptance mean with my unique set of skills and challenges today?

- "I accept the wind may frustrate me."
- "I accept my partner may have a bad day."

3. ADD PRE-ACCEPTANCE VARIABLES

Over time, **add additional variables and complexity** to your pre-acceptance practice.

For me, pre-acceptance is conscious, intentional self-talk that precedes my visualization practice (see chapter 3). My pre-acceptance practice has become more detailed and expansive over time. Initially, accepting that I didn't have control over whether I had a good or bad day felt weak, as if I were waving a white flag of defeat. I resisted pre-accepting the possibility of mistakes. As someone dedicated to perfecting my craft, I wanted perfection at all times. To really commit to pre-acceptance, I had to make myself more vulnerable and accept that I might not be able to be perfect on the day that I most desired it. Ultimately, letting go of the illusion of control to which I previously held so tightly has better positioned me to respond in real time to whatever unfolds on the court.

Pre-Acceptance and Performance Anxiety

The goal of pre-acceptance is *not* to completely eliminate stress; it is to continually lower the level of stress we experience on the court so we can improve our real-time reactions and decisions. It's like the progression of a meditation practice: at first, our minds wander after a breath or two. With practice, the mind *will still wander* (it's a mind, after all!), but we can catch it in the act and redirect it sooner rather than chasing the thought down its endless path. With pre-acceptance, in the beginning, we may only be able to successfully modulate our reaction to small triggers. Eventually, with practice and repetition, the triggers that previously plunged us into boiling water will turn up the heat more than we'd like, but we won't get burned.

I still get performance anxiety at times, and *I have no expectation that I won't.* Part of my pre-acceptance practice is knowing and accepting that I may feel tighter or more anxious than I'd like. Occasionally, during pre-match moments, my mind sometimes drifts into the what-if tide pools: "What if I disappoint my partner?" "What if my back doesn't hold up?" "What if I lose a bonus opportunity?" "What if I play poorly and my ranking drops?" I've already accepted that I may experience some anxiety; it might even be a level ten some days, but it also might be a level one. Wherever the number lands that day, I know that while it may not feel comfortable or easy, it won't break me. **Confidence in my own mental resilience**

reduces my anxiety and desire to control everything.
After a lot of practice, with increasing consistency, I
can leave the anxious ruminations off the court and
allow my training and competitive instincts to kick
into gear, letting my body do the job for which it is so
well prepared.

Pre-Acceptance and Getting the Most Out of Losses

Pre-acceptance *can* change both our experience of a
loss and, more importantly, our ability to find the lessons in the loss. Losses will still sting, but our objective
is to manage the pain of the loss in a way that doesn't
shut us down or render the information yielded by the
loss unreachable.

　　After a loss, I consciously revisit what I had
already pre-accepted. From that vantage point, I can
short-circuit the "blame and complain" game far faster
and start to mine the loss for the hidden lessons.
Nevertheless, no amount of pre-acceptance means I
am any happier or any less angry after a loss. It's still
not the time you want me as a guest at your party, but

it helps me get on track and back to work faster. It helps me wrap up my pity party and *consider* coming to your party.

Ultimately, as long as we have a brain and an ego, neither performance anxiety nor the sting of defeat is going away for good. With intentional, disciplined mental training, we can manage the magnitude of our response to the inevitable anxiety and losses that are part of every athlete's journey.

JILL

PRE-Pre-Acceptance

While watching a professional pickleball match a few weeks after my first tournament, my chest tightened as I listened to the sportscasters' commentary about a female pro who had been labeled as "overly emotional." In the game at hand, this player was not having her best day. She wore her irritation, premature sense of defeat, and disappointment like a scarlet letter, with her internal struggles telecast to her partner, the commentators, and spectators alike. The announcers pounced at the easy target, ruthlessly dissecting her game's volatility, her big emotional swings, and the effect it had on her partnership.

With horror, I imagined her hearing the commentary or seeing the footage where she rolled her eyes, sagged her shoulders, and shook her head in disdain. I have watched men on tour get bulgy veins, turn red in the face, and throw their paddles. In reaction I'd think, without any personal distress, "Take a breath, buddy." Watching this female player emotionally unravel on the court to the tune of critical commentary really struck a nerve.

I recognized the merciless disappointment rippling across her face and dripping off her shoulders because I had just experienced it on a microscale in my first piddly amateur tournament. At that tournament, long before "pre-acceptance" was a word that held any meaning to me, the most notable feature of my mental game was my hijacked nervous system: My sympathetic nervous system delivered an award-winning performance. Fight? ✓ Flight? ✓Freeze? ✓✓✓   No awards would be given, however, for the way I played pickleball that day.

During the tournament, my mind had ping-ponged between lamenting past misses and anxiously anticipating future matches, completely shutting down my ability to remain present and effectively manage the point at hand. Quickly kicked in double elimination, I left feeling that I had never really dropped into my own game and had instead been carried along in a frenetic tornado of see-ball, hit-ball. While my disappointment in my own performance may not have been visible, I was deeply frustrated by not only my physical game, but also by my inability to ever settle into a rhythm on the court.

For anyone reading this who is thinking, *Get a grip. It's just pickleball*, I agree wholeheartedly. I had been taken by surprise at my level of performance anxiety that day; while logically I knew that the tournament was completely inconsequential, my nervous system rebuked any rational messaging and hunkered down as if warding off an imminent threat. I've successfully survived birthing two children, passing the California Bar Exam, litigating complex legal battles, and parenting teenagers through a global pandemic. Given the far more stressful events I've navigated, it was equally inexplicable to me why a small-potatoes pickleball tournament could trigger this outsized response.

After that first tournament fiasco, I needed to do it again if for no other reason than to prove to myself that I could navigate a tournament better than that washout. Who wouldn't want to pay for the pleasure of more potential embarrassment and discomfort on their day off work? I hadn't started working with Dayne yet, and despite the mounting evidence that my mind was standing more in my own way than my third short drop, I was still stubbornly putting all my chips behind training my hard skills alone and hoping that my mental skills caught up on their own. I played in a few more tournaments, and through sheer repetition, my tournament nerves did improve *slightly*. While my performance anxiety was less acute with each tournament experience, I still struggled to find my groove.

Around the same time in my not-so-illustrious pickleball tournament career, I committed (for not the first time) to a daily mindfulness practice. Though I had practiced and taught yoga for years, I was far more drawn to the physical practice as a salve for my overactive mind and body. Despite all my years on the mat, I had craftily dodged incorporating much of a mindfulness practice into my life. Years ago, I had remarked to my yoga teacher that I could only calm my mind after I had exhausted my body. What was to become of me when my body was old and couldn't move as vigorously? He'd wryly suggested that hopefully I'd be wiser by then. Here I was a decade later, and while I had grown and evolved, I was shocked that the same mental habits still clung to my neural pathways like stubborn barnacles.

I was hopeful that my renewed dedication to a daily mindfulness practice would help me find my sea legs sooner at tournaments, to say nothing of the larger benefits that it might provide in the rest of my life. The next tournament rolled around. With some meditation practice under my belt, I entered the tournament with the *expectation* that I would feel calm and ready to play as if I were in a rec game.

When I stepped onto the court, the wind was swirling. My first serve sailed out. Two more unforced errors followed in rapid succession. Rather than the calm that I had planned for, my stomach clenched, my grip tightened, and my cortisol levels skyrocketed. I had planned for calm; instead, I was served chaos. At least in previous tournaments, I had come to *expect* performance anxiety.

As my body robotically tried *not to lose* game after game, I whirled through my mental Rolodex of mindfulness tricks to try to claw my way back to homeostasis. I kept coming up empty. My partner and I scraped our way through and somehow made it onto the podium, but I left with the knowledge that an ingredient (or two or three) was decidedly missing from my mental performance recipe.

Pre-Acceptance

Around this time, Dayne and I started to work together, and I had begun to put my mental training on equal footing with my physical training. With the mental performance aspects of my game moving to the front of my mind, I noticed certain patterns in tournaments that elicited a higher stress response for me. The common denominator was clear: playing against friends and in front of people I knew was my kryptonite. Like any glutton for punishment would do, I hastily signed up for a tournament in which I would play against many close friends (with a new, untested partner) in front of my coach. What could go wrong?

A couple of weeks before game time, I began to question my decision to register for the tournament. I confided in my husband that I was dreading it. I talked through my pre-tournament jitters with my favorite armchair psychologist friend and fellow pickleball zealot. Like any therapist worth her weight in salt, she asked me about my fears. How much time did she have? I was scared that playing against a good friend would spin me out so much that I would get donuted in every single game, that I would let down my new partner, and that I would be revealed to be a wretched pickleball player despite all the time I put into playing. And it would all go down in front of my coach.

My friend suggested that I imagine the worst happening and still being okay. Imagine getting donuted, disappointing my partner, playing my worst, *and* knowing that the world would still keep spinning on its axis. My anxiety level did go down. "The worst" in pickleball isn't really so bad after all, but I also had a sneaking suspicion that Dayne would not approve of this strategy.

Dayne and I happened to be meeting that week for the book. I ran my "prepare for the worst strategy" by him. He looked appalled. "Is that how you would prepare for a trial? You'd walk into the courtroom ready to get slaughtered?" Without so much as taking a breath, he added, "Please say no."

Of course that's not how I would prepare for a legal case. As an attorney, I'd try to predict all arguments, counter-arguments, and rebuttals. My mind would populate a flowchart with a series of "if → then" propositions: "If we argue x → then they argue y → then we argue z →. The "if-thens" would spread like weeds until I felt satisfied that I had prepared as thoroughly as possible. Knowing that I had done everything I possibly could to prepare provided me some semblance of calm before the storm.

After defending my worst-case scenario approach, Dayne gave me his pre-acceptance spiel. Like my initial resistance to a lot of things Dayne tells me to do, I didn't hop right on board the pre-acceptance train. My reluctance to Dayne-isms has nothing to do with Dayne and everything to do with my natural skepticism that the techniques that work for him could possibly also work for me. On the personality spectrum, some days I think that Dayne and I exist 180 degrees apart; it seems improbable that the same mental performance strategies could work for both of us when our brains seem like they came from two different species.

We are, however, undeniably aligned in our desire to control all things. Dayne *pretends* he is the biggest control freak, but we both know I win in that contest. We part ways in our risk tolerance and comfort with being seen during the "big moments." While high risk/high reward moments on public stages light up Dayne like the Rockefeller Plaza

Christmas tree, I prefer safe bets where both my errors and triumphs play out in private.

When Dayne told me that part of my pregame strategy required me to pre-accept that I may not have control over whether I had a good or bad day . . . well, that was a tough pill to swallow. Somehow it felt easier to mentally concede defeat by preparing for the worst rather than holding out the possibility of anything happening, while acknowledging that I would have limited control over which of the possibilities manifested.

As soon as I was ready to just nod my head and ignore him, he told me about the good stuff—the things I *do* get to control. Preparation. Decisions. Reactions. I could really get behind the first one. What I lack in natural talent, I've always made up for in work ethic. I had years under my belt of outpreparing my opponents. I felt less confident, however, in my ability to knock decisions and reactions out of the ballpark.

The best news is that Dayne pre-populated the answer to all the most important decisions and reactions that I would have to make. There is no one who likes a question with one right answer more than me! No matter what happened, the "then" part of the "if-then" statement always had the same answer: I won't break. Both on the pickleball court and in the matters that truly count in life, my fear

My life's worth of evidence supported his answer and not my fears: I don't break.

has always been that I would freeze or get swallowed whole by the chaos. My life's worth of evidence supported his answer and not my fears: I don't break.

With the equation that always yielded the same answer, I felt ready for the tournament. For Dayne, the pregame what-ifs take the shape of injuries, career consequences, and lost opportunities. For me, the what-ifs revolve around my ability to mentally show up and stick around for a tournament in a way that allows me to actually play my game rather than just uncomfortably survive the day. I pre-accepted the possibility of all the things that scared me and all the best possible outcomes. To my surprise, I imagined feeling resolute, unbreakable, and ready to react, decide, and respond.

The previously dreaded tournament was neither the worst nor the best of what I could have imagined. There were exciting wins and disappointing losses, but all the while my mind stayed present and engaged. Did I have pregame jitters? Certainly, but, I had already accepted that I might, and I already knew they wouldn't tank me; therefore they didn't bother me too much. I felt more performance anxiety when my opponents were good friends, but even that felt more manageable since I had pre-accepted that playing against them would be more challenging for me. Even when my partner became visibly frustrated with me, which would normally take me down the toilet, I kept redirecting my focus to my own reactions and decisions and was able to manage her irritation.

I've since played around with my pre-acceptance practice and had variable success, but the needle is consistently moving in the right direction. I land faster in games, I spin out less, and I feel better. Of course, there have also been bumps in the road, moments where I'm thinking, *Well, shoot. I didn't even think to pre-accept THAT*. Dayne and my closest friends would tell you that I show up differently now on the court. I look taller or feistier or something *more*. Dayne likes to say that it's like

I got abducted by an alien, had a brain transplant, and was dropped back on the pickleball court. Truthfully, it feels that way sometimes.

3

SEE AND FEEL
YOUR GAME

DAYNE

I'm hiding in the far corner of the locker room by the showers that no longer work, trying to remain invisible while I complete my pre-match visualization routine. I can hear other players walking in and out, one muttering under his breath to himself about a loss, another talking about his game plan for his next match, and another complaining about his partner. I'm nervously sitting on the cold steel bench, hands on my knees, head down, eyes closed, with a towel draped over my head and neck. The darkness I've created drops me into a new quiet state; where once I could hear every word of the athletes coming and going, I now hear nothing. The locker room is mine: just me and my visuals of the next match.

I play an entire game in my mind's eye—every third shot, dinking pattern, attack, counterattack, and reset. I see my two opponents clear as day in my head. I feel their nerves, weaknesses, and vulnerabilities rising with each point while my confidence grows. My nerves begin to turn into belief as my breath slows and my body relaxes. It's happening exactly as I want; my mind and body are aligning, ready to compete at the highest level.

The game I'm playing out in my mind methodically progresses to match point. I serve from the left side and hit a low, stinging topspin third shot drive, which is returned to my backhand in the middle of the transition zone. My fifth shot is an easy drop, seamlessly getting us to the kitchen line. After the fifteenth dink, I initiate an attack on the opponent in front of me. He counter-attacks, and I slide to the left to hit a heavy topspin forehand at his feet, which he's forced to reset, popping the ball up too high to sit perfectly for my two-handed backhand. I slam my backhand for the match-ending winner down the center of the court. The match is ours. I calmly turn to my partner, paddle tap, and walk to the net and paddle tap our opponents.

I slowly take a couple of deep breaths, open my eyes, and take the towel off my head when I hear someone yell across the locker room from the entrance: "Dayne, you in here? We're up. Let's go!" That's how every tournament begins for me. Before my paddle touches the ball, I've already seen and felt each point, game, and match.

Before my paddle touches the ball, I've already seen and felt each point, game, and match.

Using visualization—the creation of a detailed image of what you want to happen—to enhance physical and mental performance isn't new in the world of athletic performance. Athletes and coaches have been using visualization, imagery, and guided meditation as training tools to learn new skills, better execute skills, and maintain calm and focus under competitive stress for years. Yet in the pickleball world, most coaching and instruction has leaned into optimizing performance through the mastery of technique and mechanics alone. The overemphasis on mechanics is particularly misplaced in pickleball, which allows for greater variability and creativity in how to get the job done than in many other sports. This chapter explores the how and why of incorporating visualization into training on and off the court to improve the micro of physical shot execution and the macro of mental performance under competitive stress.

The Micro: Using Visualization for Shot Execution

If you spend ten minutes online searching "how to improve your third shot drop," virtually every video tutorial you find will offer technical instruction promising a consistent drop through some magical combination of footwork, body position, wrist mechanics, and grip strength. Yet despite access to "optimal technique," most amateurs focused on mechanics alone struggle to consistently execute this seemingly simple shot. Their problem isn't that they have bad information, and the solution isn't searching out better or different techniques. The problem instead comes from overreliance on proper technique itself, which falls flat under competitive stress. To perform under competitive stress, we need to shift our focus away from mechanics and incorporate visualization—*seeing and feeling the shot*—into our training and performance.

Visualization Versus Mechanics

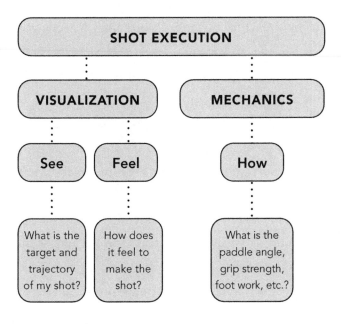

Whereas mechanics rely on the "how-to" of each shot (think grip strength, paddle angle, foot work), visualization shifts the mind's focus to *seeing* and *feeling* the shot we want to make. To train visualization, we need to hand the reins over to our "mind's eye" and "feel mind," trusting that our bodies will be able to execute our vision without specific instructions on how to do it. Rather than focusing on form, visualization comes from continually asking "see" and "feel" questions: What is my exact target for the ball? What does the trajectory of the ball look like? How does it feel to execute the shot?"

The beginning stages of visualization are very deliberate. We intentionally redirect our focus to envisioning the path of the ball over and over again. Eventually, after training our vision, our sense of feel (how our body feels as we execute the shot) will naturally follow. At that point, we no longer need to consciously visualize our shots and can rely on our "feel" mind. Ultimately, the goal is to get out of the "how-to" mind and let the "feel" mind take over, freeing up our conscious mind to engage in a higher level of strategy.

When I was teaching tennis years ago, I started experimenting with coaching novice players to use visualization skills. One afternoon, I was giving a lesson to a twelve-year-old who had never hit a tennis ball before. When we got on the court, I simplified my mechanical instruction to the most basic foundational skills: I only taught her how to grip the racquet and swing it through the air so she wouldn't hurt her arm. Standing on opposite service lines, I asked her to hit the ball to me. The only instruction was to aim the ball *at me* without worrying about how high or hard to hit the ball. She asked me all the mechanical questions that instinctively came to her, but I assured her we would get to that later. The ball didn't always cross the net and just as often hit the back fence, but it always came *toward* me, never straying too far to the left or right of me. Her body was able to intuitively figure out how to organize itself to hit the ball toward me without telling her about the "proper" point of contact, direction of her racquet face, or her stance.

After experiencing the benefit of visualization in tennis, incorporating the same coaching practices into pickleball, a sport far less dependent on precise mechanics than tennis, was a no-brainer. In pickleball, visualization prompts for a 3.5 player trying to improve the third shot drop might sound like this:

Visualization Prompts for the Third Drop Shot

SEE
- What does the "baby arc" of the ball's trajectory look like coming off the paddle?
- How softly does the ball cross the top of the net?

FEEL
- How still and balanced does your body feel at contact?
- What does the paddle feel like in your hand?

Like the progression from drawing a stick figure to painting a landscape, as we progress, our visualization can become increasingly granular, including additional details, such as the trajectory, spin, and pace of the ball.

There is no "right way" to visualize, and how we envision the shape of our shots will vary among athletes. When I visualize, I see an imaginary laser beam tracking the trajectory of the ball as it leaves my paddle and travels to my target. While most athletes can envision a ball's trajectory moving from their paddle to a spot on the court, not all can. For those athletes, leaning directly into their feel sense is more effective. (How does my body *feel* when I successfully execute this shot?) That said, if you think you cannot "see" with the mind's eye, I'd offer that you are doing it all the time, whether you realize it or not. Have you ever purposefully hit a pickleball to an open space? If so, take a moment to consider what your brain has to do to hit a tiny ball with a tiny paddle to a tiny spot on a tiny court where your opponent can't hit it. It's insanely difficult to do if you are consciously thinking about it. Before you sell yourself short, remind yourself you may already be using visualization without even knowing it.

The biggest challenge of prioritizing visualization over mechanics is managing the fear of getting it wrong. Learning through visualization and feel requires zero judgment over "failed" shot execution and a recognition of the value of short-term failures. As a coach, it's my job to continually redirect my students' focus away

The biggest challenge of prioritizing visualization over mechanics is managing the fear of getting it wrong.

from the short-term result and back to questioning, "What does the shot look like? What does it feel like?"

If you can tolerate the short-term errors, mastering a shot through vision and feel offers more consistency under competitive stress in the long term. Under competitive stress, mechanics tend to falter because they require us to be consciously thoughtful about how to execute a shot rather than trusting that our body knows what to do. When we become consciously thoughtful, we are more likely to tense up, make errors, and mute our mind's ability to engage in the higher-level strategic thinking required in a game. Moreover, when our attention is overly focused on individual shot execution, we are often blinded to the shot patterns playing out in front of us that are essential to solving the strategic puzzle that brought us to the court in the first place. When we let feel and visualization guide our shots, we open the mental bandwidth to see the bigger picture and adjust to the game that is unfolding in front of us.

The ultimate challenge? How do I hit the mechanic I want without consciously thinking of how to perform the mechanic? Proper mechanics are obviously important, but to achieve them, we need to focus on something completely different than the mechanics we're trying to learn. **The magic happens when we use visualization as a back door into the mechanics we are trying to execute, which helps eliminate the conscious thought patterns that inhibit performance.**

The lure of learning through technique alone is strong as it lends itself to external verification. We can see with our eyes whether we are locking the wrist, contacting the ball in front of us, and keeping the paddle face open. There is visual evidence of attaining mechanical progression. We can watch a video of ourselves practicing a physical technique and immediately confirm whether we are using the mechanics that we have been taught. That demonstrable and instant feedback is the addictive agent of mechanics.

Visualization and feel are subjective. If we were to film ourselves drilling while using visualization and feel to guide our shots, we can't "see" the difference in our "feel" and "vision" in the instances that our shots hit or fell flat. Other than seeing a progression in our shot over time, we can't externally verify that we are "doing it right." Since our minds prefer certainty, we often will instinctively migrate to the verifiable *how to make* the shot rather than the *invisible look and feel* of the shot.

The Macro: Incorporating Visualization off the Court

On the court, we use visuals to give the mind enough data to produce the shot that we have envisioned. Off the court, we can use visualization to both hone individual shots and execute entire points, games, and matches from our mind's eye. Because visualization happens in our mind, we can play light years faster than the time it takes to physically manifest a point or game.

Off-court visualization can be done anywhere and anytime regardless of weather, court availability, or injuries. Creating a visualization practice is simply a matter of prioritizing it. In 2020, I injured my back and was sidelined from the pickleball court for four months. While I was recovering, I poured my attention into visualization. After many sedentary months, I eased my way back onto the court with a morning on the ball machine. My body was deconditioned and tight from months of quiet recovery. Fifteen minutes into my session, once I had shaken off the rust, I realized that I hadn't missed a beat in the execution of the shots that I had been visualizing. If anything, my mind felt sharper, and my aim, trajectory, and spin were clicking into place as if I had doubled down on drilling for the past four months. I paused the feed on my ball machine.

How could I possibly feel better after four months without so much as touching a ball? I had been coaching about the power of visualization for thirty years but was still stunned by its potency. There was no way that I should have been able to step back on the court with more accuracy and precision than before I got hurt, but I had put in hours of making the perfect shot, setting up points, and closing games. I hadn't made a bad shot or poor strategic decision in my mind's eye over those four grueling months.

That's what visualization offers that can never be replicated in a physical practice: you don't ever have to make a mistake. In your mind's eye, you can make limitless perfect shots, construct unbeatable points, and mentally and physically dominate every game and match. You not only get the reps of your

In your mind's eye, you can make limitless perfect shots, construct unbeatable points, and mentally and physically dominate every game and match.

visualization, but you get *perfect* reps. When we can get out of our own way by taming our overactive mind and developing confidence in our body's ability to actualize the shot we've envisioned, our potential becomes limitless.

Visualization Exercise
How to Visualize a Point, Game, and Match

Developing a visualization practice takes time and repetition. Start simple. Begin by visualizing one point with as much detail as possible. Once it becomes natural to incorporate granular detail into each point, expand your visualization to play multiple points. Eventually, grow your practice to include an entire game and match.

See and Feel Your Game

1. Find a comfortable position and close your eyes. Slow your breath, bringing intention to your inhale and exhale.

2. Begin by visualizing a point in which you are the server. Before you serve, feel the pickleball in your hand, noting its grittiness and holes. Take in your surroundings: Are there games being played next to you? Can you hear balls being hit and players talking and laughing? You're not being distracted by the outside noise, just acknowledging its reality.

3. Toss the ball and hit an aggressive serve. Visualize its spin, trajectory, pace, and landing target. Watch your serve jump up into your opponent's paddle. Visualize his return of serve in granular detail.

4. Visualize you and your partner move as a connected team. See your opponents' response to your shots.

5. With this same level of clarity and detail, play the rest of the point out in your mind remembering that every ball you hit is intentional and perfectly placed. After several shots back and forth, close the point with a winner.

6. As you become more skilled in your visualization, begin playing multiple points, both as the serving and receiving team, eventually progressing to a full game.

7. Before a tournament, play out match point. Play the point in two different ways, but always end with hitting the last ball for a winner. Continue the visualization through the celebration of tapping paddles or hugging your partner. Instead of simply seeing the win in your mind, feel the excitement of the win.

JILL

I am a very left-brain gal. I color within the lines, I prefer rules to chaos, and love a well-crafted set of step-by-step instructions. In law school, when I learned the entire body of law neatly fit into an endless outline, my brain was in heaven. My first attraction to yoga mistakenly came from the idea that there was a "right" way to do each pose. A set of rules and instructions that, if you followed carefully with diligence over time, allowed you to achieve perfection. (Of course, yoga isn't really about that at all, but it took years of practicing for me to figure that out.) I'm an East Coaster by origin, born to computer scientists in a family where we like things we can see with our real eyes. If you said things like "mind's eye" and "feel-mind" in my house, you'd be shipped right off to live with the hippies in California.

Dayne, on the other hand, is a right-brain kind of guy. As a kid, he practiced sports with a whole team of imaginary teammates and opponents. I imagine his inner world looks a lot like that of the lady in *The Queen's Gambit*, inhabited by moves and counterattacks against imaginary foes. It made plenty of sense that visualization would work for a creative mind like his, but based on my learning preferences, I'd prefer a tidy set of instructions. What business did this square brain have trying to fit into an imaginary circle? Finally, without a racquet background, I often felt I had started the pickleball racecourse ten miles behind all those pesky tennis players and needed more mechanics instruction than those who already knew what to do with a paddle and ball.

My initial assumption that technique-based instruction would benefit me has been repeatedly challenged over the last two years. I've experimented with all different ways of learning a shot, often zigzagging back and forth between obsessing over technique and completely letting vision and feel guide my process, ultimately arriving at my own mishmash style of learning.

Phase I: All Mechanics, All the Time

In my early days on the pickleball court, the third shot drop had eluded mastery for me despite repetition, clinics, temper tantrums, and yet more repetition. She had been a fickle lady in my game— coming, going, mysteriously returning, only to leave again. Some games, some days, even in some high-stress moments, my drops landed perfectly. What made those sublime drop days different from the dark ones was a complete mystery to me. On the latter, my mind immediately searched for a technical solution: Maybe I wasn't meeting the ball in front of me? Overswinging? Over-gripping? Moving while I made contact? So many ways to get it wrong! The biggest problem was that I had no idea what I was doing differently between when my drop landed and when it faltered.

I watched so many YouTube video tutorials. So. Many. Videos. Before meeting Dayne, I even shopped my drop problem around with different coaches. With each successive lesson, all with solid technique coaching, my drop became increasingly unpredictable. My best friend summed it up:

"Whenever anyone messes with your drop, it gets worse and worse. Just leave it alone already!"

Phase II: Dipping My Pinky Toe into Visualization (Then Yanking It out Again)

Never one to say "uncle," I eventually took a lesson with Dayne as a last-gasp effort to "fix" my much-maligned drop. The lesson was completely different from my previous ones. Rather than offering technical advice, Dayne directed my attention to where I was hitting the ball, what the ball's arc would look like as it crested the net, and how my body felt when I made the shot. Not a word was whispered about my form or technique. There was a lot of talk about the baby rainbow arc of the drop and the imaginary laser tracing the ball's trajectory as it left my paddle. You know, the rantings of a visualization zealot. Dayne's reliance on seeing and feeling the shot was backed by his unwavering confidence in our body and our mind's ability to adjust and configure themselves with good visual and sensory inputs. While I had my doubts about trying to see and feel my way through my third shot drop, in the most surprising way my drop slowly started to take the shape that I was aiming for, coming closer and closer to landing in the spot I envisioned. The hour lesson was a mash-up of complete discomfort and total ease.

From that day forward, was it all third shot drops that perfectly crested over the net to land out of the reach of even my longest opponents? Not quite. For about two weeks afterward, my drops were consistent. I didn't have to apologize to my partner for setting us up for a smash ball for fourteen days! It was glorious. But then, as mysteriously as my drop showed up, it left again. It seemed that the further that Dayne's steady drumbeat of vision/feel faded from my mind, the more dysregulated my drop became. When I told myself to see and feel the shot without Dayne's confidence in my ability to execute the shot, my vision felt obscured by my fear of missing the drop again, as if my magical drop powers had been neutralized by my own doubts.

In my lesson, I had benefited from Dayne's relentless positive reinforcement and ability to be nonplussed by my errors. His confidence in my body's ability to figure out what to do was an effective proxy for my own skepticism. He kept my fear of failed execution and self-doubt at bay, which allowed me to calm down enough to trust myself. Without him around and my fierce inner critic back out in full force, I struggled to regain the ability to see and feel the shot that had taken up temporary residence in my mind for those two weeks. Having lost confidence in visualization, I beat a hasty retreat to the safe haven of mechanics, frequently returning to technique videos after a particularly rough day.

Phase III: Wading Deeper into Vision

Fast-forward through hundreds of apologies to my partners for the balls that rained down upon us following one of my dreaded pop-ups, and I was back in a lesson with Dayne. I wasn't willing to spend yet another lesson with him on my drop. That finicky gal had usurped enough of my time and attention for a lifetime. This time, I wanted to learn the top spin roller attack. With no experience generating top spin, it seemed like prime territory for a good old-fashioned lesson in technique. Annoyingly, Dayne asked me to show him the shot I wanted him to show me. That guy! I hit a series of rollers into the net. Now's the time you might think he would make some technical correction. You'd be wrong.

Instead, he asked me to watch him hit three rollers that went into the net as mine had, followed by three well-executed rollers. Then he challenged me to "spot the difference" between the two sets. I particularly appreciated the comical component of this teaching method: "This is what you're doing [imagine flailing shot execution]." "Now watch this [imagine graceful shot execution]." Then, without uttering a word about technique or adjusting my grip or paddle face, he asked me to try again. To my surprise, my roller quickly began to find its way over the net and hasn't left my side since.

Phase IV: Finding the Connection Between Self-Belief and Visualization

For anyone keeping track of my record for learning through visualization and feel, Team See/Feel had one win (roller) and one draw (drop). I wanted to expand my sample size and put another shot through the how-I-learn-best test: the forehand push slice dink. When I asked to learn that dink, I specifically requested that he teach me the mechanics of the shot. He isn't anti-mechanics, so he obliged. He showed me how to hold the paddle and use my arm as a level without getting too wristy. It all felt so good . . . until I tried it on my own the next day. Despite my success in the lesson, with my drilling partner only twenty-four hours later, my slices were flying high as I tried to make my wrist into the shape Dayne had shown me.

My drilling partner, who had limitless patience for my verbalization of all my pickleball thoughts, considerately listened as I tried to explain to him what I thought I was supposed to do. My description included unhelpful images: "I feel like my wrist is supposed to look like a dinosaur."

My partner supportively nodded with a raised eyebrow. Eventually, I put us both out of our misery and retired my poor T-Rex slice. The next week, I asked Dayne to adjust my wrist position again. He obliged—again. This time, I was so locked up trying to "make this shape" with my wrist that I felt like a rusty dinosaur robot hacking at the ball. Then I thought back to my prior roller lesson and just watched Dayne for a while. I stopped focusing on paddle angle, elbows, wrists, and shoulders, letting my body mimic what I saw. Poof! The slice was back. After dinking back and forth for a while, Dayne stopped and asked, "What just happened? What changed?" I said something insightful like, "I dunno."

Now that Team See/Feel had racked up another win, I wanted to understand why visualization worked well for learning the slice dink but hadn't had the same lasting success with my drop. I started thinking about teaching yoga and how my teaching had evolved over the years. When I was a newer teacher, my teaching was littered with precise, detailed cues to get my students into the "right" alignment, engaging the "right" muscles, and breathing at the "right" time. Though not consciously, my teaching rested on the assumption that unless I told students exactly how to move, they couldn't figure out how to safely arrange their bodies. As I became more confident in the intelligence of bodies and the value I offered as an instructor without dumping my "knowledge" on my students, I let go of my unnecessarily fussy cuing and trusted my students could figure out the way their bodies wanted to hold poses. Often, the less I said, the more efficiently and effectively my students were able to navigate the complex movements that had previously eluded them.

It struck me that while I had craved mechanics instruction in my early days on the court and believed it was the only way I could learn certain shots, I had long ago abandoned the equivalent teaching philosophy in yoga. When I considered the different shots I had learned through the lens of my teaching experience, my learning experiences made much more sense: the more I was able to trust that my body could figure out how to execute a shot without detailed instructions, the better my body was able to learn to feel the shot.

With a cleaner mental slate and boatloads more confidence in my body's ability to figure things out, I revisited my drop. Over a year had passed, so my drop had become better through sheer grinding and repetition, but there were still refinements I wanted to make. This time, I drew on what had worked for me with the roller and slice: rather than envisioning the trajectory of the ball, watching others execute a shot was the best back door into "seeing and feeling" the shot for me. I picked a few professional players and watched them drop in slow motion over and over and over. I went out with my ball machine and tried to approximate what I had seen. Then I asked Dayne to weigh in. Luckily, he used my very favorite teaching technique: "Here's what you're doing. Here's what you should be doing." I filmed his imitations of current-me and the new-improved-future-me and then marinated. My forehand drop slowly began to step back in line. It isn't perfect and continues to cause me occasional angst, but accessing the shot through my body rather than my mind has provided a far more reliable portal to consistently execute the shot than my months of tortured mechanics analysis. Besides, given what an overactive thinker I am, I love every moment of letting my body do its thing and giving my brain a day off.

4

CHOOSE CONFIDENCE

JILL

ONE AFTERNOON AT OPEN play, I was partnered with a lovely woman, who in my estimation was playing well. Every time she missed a shot, however, her body sagged like a marionette who had lost its puppeteer. You could see her confidence draining with each point like a bucket springing successively more leaks. In between matches, she lamented that she was in a "slump." She had "lost" her game somewhere, somehow. But where had it gone, and how could she find it? As if she had dropped her keys in the sand, the more furiously she searched for her game, the more elusive and buried it became. Before she finished describing her pickleball woes, she interrupted herself to say, "This needs to be a chapter in the book. Tell me how to get out of this."

My game was no Rock of Gibraltar, marked by improbable highs and inexplicable lows. Like my friend, the dips in my game boggled me and reminded me of an uninvited house guest: *Why did you show up now? How long do you plan to stay?* I was on board to have Dayne tell us how to usher these unwanted visitors to the door, post-haste. I was imagining an action plan—a step-by-step guide of how to break a slump and maybe how to prevent one altogether. I texted Dayne about our new chapter subject. Per our usual process of creating a chapter, I then sent him a series of questions about slumps and patiently waited to discuss them.

Weeks later at our meeting, I cracked open my laptop, ready to receive the secrets to a slump-free life. As Dayne sat down, I turned on my recorder, but before I could get the first question out, he said, "I don't believe in slumps." I may as well have tasked myself with writing a profile of the Easter Bunny, only to learn he wasn't real. The recording of our conversation would suggest that I blurted out, "Well *that* would have been helpful to know before we met."

Overly attached to my meticulously planned questions, I pushed back. Athletes experience slumps all the time, right? I'd heard sports commentators talk about them; I'd watched friends suffer through them; I'd gone through them—or at least I thought I had. Perhaps we were simply talking past one another and language, rather than the concept, was the problem? "Haven't you coached athletes who perceive they are in a rut?" I pressed. Of course he had; clients didn't seek him out because they were playing at peak performance. Hoping to salvage our meeting time, I asked, "So what do you call *that*?" "I call it normal," he said. Substituting in "normal" for "slump" in my questions produced a nonsensical Mad Libs-like inquisition. Our meeting and chapter were on the verge of their very own slump.

Unwilling to call time of death on my original vision of the chapter, I tried bargaining: "Would you agree to call it *shaken confidence*?" He tepidly agreed. Like a forced march in bare feet over gravel, we uncomfortably trudged through my questions. Later on, having gotten almost nowhere for the price of our discomfort, I eventually realized that I was asking the wrong questions. The only two questions left were, "If we are discussing a concept that has no value, why are we still discussing it?" And, "If slumps don't exist, then why do so many of us think we have been in one?"

DAYNE

As I taught a doubles clinic a couple of years back, I could feel my phone continuously vibrating in my pocket. After the third call, I interrupted the clinic to check my phone, praying it wasn't a family emergency. A young male pro I had been coaching had left me *eight* voicemails. I returned the phone to my pocket and finished the clinic, but my curiosity was piqued. The second the clinic was over, I listened to all of them.

Each message sounded the same: "Dayne, I suck! I've been working my butt off every day, but I still can't win a big tournament match. I've been in a slump for over a month and am thinking about quitting." He was focusing on singles, hoping to differentiate himself on the singles circuit to help attract a good doubles partner. Convinced that his short-term stumbles were going to sink his long-term success, he was panicked. He mentioned the word *slump* multiple times, believing his current state of struggle would dictate his future.

When we got on the phone, instead of fighting him on whether he was in a slump, I simply agreed with him. The only way we would find solutions together and shift his fear into confidence was to help him see that his fears were normal and experienced by many athletes during the learning process.

Eventually, as we normalized his fears, I could feel him exhale with relief, at which point we could lean into his preparation and training and the confidence that they could create in the long term. We slowly chipped away at his fear of losing in the short term and created a deeper understanding that today's losses, or poor play, is a normal and natural ebb in the growth process. **Instead of focusing on the self-fulfilling prophecy of a slump, we trained his mind to shift to the reward that inevitably shows up on the other side of short-term struggles.**

A few months after working with him, he texted me after a huge singles win over a top player: "Dayne, I lost a close one in the gold—a match I should've won—but I can feel the growth. The preparation I've put in this last month is paying off, and I guarantee I'll be pulling out these types of matches soon."

Why Slumps Don't Exist

Debunking the idea of a slump is key to successfully navigating normal variations in our performance. The very notion that slumps are a phenomena that plagues athletes is the most dangerous thing about them. When the pro singles player I coached interpreted his normal variance in performance as a slump, he became trapped in a losing mental loop, creating a powerful self-fulfilling prophecy. To shake the slump, he had to wrest his confidence from his temporary disappointing results and commit to a macro vision of his trajectory, undaunted by micro dips in performance.

The idea of a slump is based on the fallacy that there is something abnormal or noteworthy about ebbs and flows in your game. Even the best athletes on the planet have variations in their day-to-day, week-to-week, or even month-to-month performance. No matter our talent, preparation, and focus, every day, week, or month will not be our best. As soon as we label

As soon as we label a regular variation a deviant event, we exponentially increase the probability that it will become a self-fulfilling prophecy.

a regular variation a deviant event (such as branding an off-week or month a slump), we exponentially increase the probability that it will become a self-fulfilling prophecy. Insecurity or a lack of belief in our ability to perform is anathema to optimal performance. Deciding that a normal fluctuation in play is a slump only acts to amplify any underlying dip in confidence that is hindering our performance in the first place. **Fluctuations in our play don't deserve a name more noteworthy than normal, super normal, expected, or being human.** That said, if you insist on framing ebbs and flows in your game as pathological events rather than healthy variance, you can rest assured that you are creating the optimal mental environment for a slump to flourish.

If we pull back the curtain, a slump rests on the following false conditional statements:

- If my results are good → my confidence is high.
- When/Once I play better → I will be/ can be/deserve to be confident.

Tying self-belief to performance invites a confidence death spiral. **When confidence flows *from* performance, a regular fluctuation in play can rattle self-belief, welcoming in the next bad moment.** It's like hooking our confidence to a tripwire that we know will get triggered time and time again, often during the make-or-break moments.

The Antidote: Unconditional Confidence

The antidote is flipping the script and retaking control of our confidence from our results. Repeat after me: **Confidence is not conditional**. Get out your Sharpie or head to the tattoo parlor. I want your nondominant forearm to read: **Confidence is a decision, not a result.** Every time you serve the ball, recommit to the idea that your self-belief is fixed, known, and invariable, whatever follows in that point, game, or match.

At first glance, confidence that isn't grounded in, or exceeds the reality of, our performance sounds like it's creeping into the dangerous territory of arrogance. Unconditional confidence, however, is a different beast than arrogance. Arrogance is loud, brash, and in your face. The arrogant athlete is devoid of true confidence and compensates for his lack of belief by telling you how good he is. The very fact he has to *say* it means he doesn't *know it* and might not even think or believe it.

Unconditional confidence is backed by the *unspoken knowledge* that you are unbreakable. It replaces uncertain *belief* with unshakeable *knowledge*. With the same certitude you know the sky is blue, you *know* you are better prepared than anyone on the court. No matter the score or micro-swings, you *know* you won't break. Unconditional confidence is quiet, intimidating, and mysterious and is a prerequisite for achievement at the highest levels.

While we can see the advantage of unshakable, even excessive self-belief in others, many of us aren't willing to allow ourselves the same benefit. We either don't think we deserve it or fear it will steal our drive to grind. Let's put both of those misconceptions to rest.

First, depriving ourselves of unconditional confidence because we believe we haven't "earned it" mixes up the order of operations and places confidence as the *product* of performance rather than the *multiplier*. We can solidify our confidence through our work habits, preparation, and mindset, but we don't "earn it" through our performance.

Second, **unconditional confidence, when paired with humility, creates a positive feedback loop that fuels our drive rather than dampens it**. Athletes get into trouble when they couple their confidence with *entitlement*, a toxic combination that has derailed many talented athletic careers, including my own. As a young tennis and basketball player, my exaggerated sense of my own abilities, and what was owed to me because of them, deluded me into believing that I was exempt from putting in the hard work. I wrongly believed that my natural talent would not only carry me, but also entitled me to success. My conceit cost me athletic scholarships, the opportunity to play collegiate sports, and success at higher levels as a professional tennis player. Wondering "what could have been" would still haunt me if those stinging lost opportunities hadn't taught me humility, which was woefully absent in my younger self. The athlete I am today and my commitment to being the hardest working player on the senior pro circuit was born not from my successes, but from those painful losses.

Though seemingly contradictory, **our mental and physical performance thrive when humility**

and massive self-belief coexist in a teeter-totter of constant equilibration. The challenge becomes learning how to effectively toggle between the two. Off the court, humility rules the roost. Whereas arrogance threatens to breed complacency, humility is the powerhouse of preparation and training. Without the humility to recognize that we can lose to any player, we risk losing the discipline to put in the extra hours of training and preparation that feeds our confidence.

Going into tournaments, we have to both be all alpha *and* all underdog. Every time I step on the court, I know *both* that I can beat anyone *and* that I could be beaten by anyone. If I don't believe I can outplay anyone on the court, how can I possibly make it happen? If I don't believe with equal force that I could be beat, I risk becoming cocky and losing my focus and intensity. Like so many elements of building a strong mental game, striking the right balance between humility and unconditional confidence is a delicate dance that requires experimentation, failure, patience, and practice. I've tipped too far on both sides of the scale and paid for it. When the balance is right, however, it's like finding the keys to the castle of peak performance.

Cultivating Unconditional Confidence

Unconditional confidence isn't easy, instantaneous, or self-perpetuating. When I say "decide" to be confident, I mean decide *and* then nurture your confidence with the physical and mental work it needs to grow. There isn't a fixed formula, but the most mentally robust athletes with whom I've worked cultivate confidence by:

> **Unconditional confidence isn't easy, instantaneous, or self-perpetuating.**

1. Committing to preparation and training
2. Learning to quickly release errors and refocus on the next point
3. Choosing confidence despite normal fluctuations in performance

Unconditional Confidence

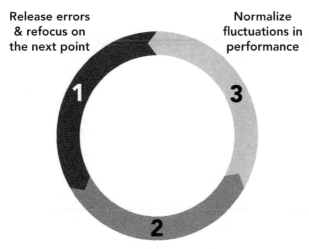

Release errors
& refocus on
the next point

Normalize
fluctuations in
performance

Commit to preparation
& training

1. Commit to Preparation & Training

Unconditional confidence is anchored in preparation and training, which direct the mind's focus toward "What can I do now?" and away from past performance or future outcomes. They are the ultimate variables within your control, not only shoring up your physical game but battle-readying your mind. If you have left no stone unturned in your preparation, the very knowledge of your exhaustive training will help effectively manage your on-court reactions and decisions. To know that you have out-trained your opponents is to *know* you won't break first.

How you train is as important as whether or not you train. Filling your schedule with rec games, especially if you are winning them all, will do little to shore up your mental and physical game. Skills and confidence are built through drilling, repping on the wall or with the ball machine, and taking risks in rec games to hone new skills and strategies. Training that is comfortable and easy will not yield the mental and physical skills needed to compete in the higher-intensity tournament environment. Just like you wouldn't train at sea-level for a race at ten thousand feet, your preparation won't serve you if it is free from any intensity or competitive stress. Like building any muscle, place enough stress on your training so that your confidence can learn to accommodate the load.

2. Release Errors and Refocus on the Next Point

Tell me how you respond to errors, and I'll tell you whether you'll spend more time on Team Ebb or Team

Flow. Response to errors, whether our own or our partner's, dictates the resilience of our performance. Mentally strong players respond efficiently and proactively to errors; the last shot is released, allowing the next shot to take center stage. These solution-oriented athletes clear errors like scribbles on an Etch A Sketch, a quick shake dissolving what was and priming the board for what comes next.

In mentally untrained athletes, errors take on the quality of wet tar, trapping the mind's focus in the error. Once the mind's spotlight gets fixated on fear of making subsequent errors, our mindset subtly shifts from playing *to win* to playing *not to lose*. Each subsequent shot, both in execution and selection, unconsciously becomes a hedged bet in a self-defeating bid to stave off subsequent errors. Rather than protecting against more errors, often the opposite happens, creating a cascade of underperformance. Ultimately, **when we unconsciously hand the reins of our mindset over to our performance, any given error threatens to catapult us out of our flow and into counterproductive self-preservation mode**.

Because of the rapid momentum swings in pickleball games, if we don't find a way to minimize negativity after a miss, a game can get away from us quickly. Developing a reset ritual that allows us to let go of the last point and anchor our focus on the next is a critical skill for stopping game-ending runs and getting back into the driver's seat. While there isn't a switch to flip, we can shift our response to errors through conscious practice. After all, an error is just an error until we choose to attach significance to it.

An error is just an error until we choose to attach significance to it.

After a bad miss, I allow myself to emotionally react because if I don't, I'll explode later. I immediately turn my back to my opponents, slow down my walk, elongate my breathing, go to the back fence, and repeat a specific sentence to myself. Before I turn around, I have a physical trigger that aligns my mental game with my composure reset. This ensures that I've "let go" of the last miss and am fully locked in to the next point.

Some pros tap the back fence. Others reset with more complex physical and mental routines. Whatever the technique, the goal is to intentionally separate the last point from the next. The process of resetting mentally and emotionally is an individual one. It might take some tinkering to find your reset routine, but it's helpful to start simple:

Example Routine to Release an Error & Refocus on the Next Point

1. **RELEASE FRUSTRATION**

2. **SLOW YOUR WALK**

3. **SLOW YOUR BREATH**

4. **SAY RESET MANTRA TO SELF**

A reset mantra can be as simple as "THIS point." Alternatively, you choose a more forceful refrain that envisions errors as opportunities to up your play. Replace "I can't make another mistake!" with "Let's go! These moments are why I play." With discipline and repetition, your chosen response will eventually take root and become your reflexive one.

Athletes frequently see their own punishing thoughts as a penance they are taking alone, but nothing is further from the truth. How you respond to errors can either fortify your partnership or take it down the tubes. Unless you have the world's best poker face, **your response to missed points and errors is a highly contagious agent that will infect your partner.** If you spin out in response to dips in play, your partner must allocate energy either to buoying you or blocking out your negativity, which threatens to break the energetic connection in the partnership. As a good partner, it's your

> If you spin out in response to dips in play, your partner must allocate energy either to buoying you or blocking out your negativity, which threatens to break the energetic connection in the partnership.

obligation to learn to manage your response to errors and stay mentally present for the next point.

3. Choose Confidence and Normalize Fluctuations in Performance

Detaching your confidence from fluctuations in performance isn't a one-time decision. Unconditional confidence must be nourished by daily actions. Because performance will vary from day to day and week to week, without a consistent way of insulating your confidence from the natural vicissitudes in your play, your self-belief will naturally start to rise and fall with your ebbs and flows. To protect against this inclination, incorporate a ritualized way of reinforcing your confidence:

Rituals to Reinforce Unconditional Confidence

 VISUAL RITUAL

Put up a sticky note with a confidence-affirming mantra that you'll see every day.

 SELF-TALK RITUAL

Incorporate a confidence-affirming mantra into your self-talk rituals.

 VISUALIZATION RITUAL

See yourself with impermeable confidence as part of your visualization practice.

 WARM-UP RITUAL

Incorporate a confidence-affirming mantra into your on-court warm-up routine.

Maintaining unconditional confidence as an athlete is a lifelong process and challenges even the most seasoned professionals. Armed with the knowledge that there are actionable steps you can take to resuscitate flagging self-belief can help you reverse a normal dip in performance. If your confidence falters, then take a breath and remind yourself that fluctuations in performance are to be expected, and know that you have all the tools you need to reestablish your self-belief.

JILL

As I listened to Dayne's anti-slump stump speech at lunch that day, my response spanned the spectrum from intrigued to skeptical. On the one hand, it felt freeing to consider a pickleball world in which a slump wasn't lurking behind a net post, waiting to jump out and sabotage my game for the next week or month. The idea of detaching my confidence from my performance sounded heavenly and something that I would buy at full price with overnight shipping if one could order such a thing. On the other hand, aspects of Dayne's advice struck me as something that might work for others but not me.

My brain is a stubborn mule and often ignores what I tell it to do. I've told my brain not to worry so much for almost five decades, and low and behold, that worry machine seems to run on a mind of its own, immune to my conscious directives. While I desperately wanted to *decide* that my confidence would not be dictated by my performance, I truthfully wondered whether that was something I was capable of *deciding*, even if I outtrained every person to have picked up a pickleball paddle.

I didn't mention my reticence to Dayne that day. Instead, we talked about the recent ebbs and flows in my game and the factors that seemed to influence my performance. Unfortunately, what caused my highs and lows was still shrouded in mystery to me. I had just experienced both a long, glorious period of elevated performance, followed by a far less enjoyable month-long dip in my play. It was the perfect field to mine for clues into what invoked the best and worst in my performance and whether "deciding" to be unconditionally confident was a viable strategy for me. In grim detail, I recounted my most recent roller-coaster performance ride to Dayne:

My period of peak performance, I explained, followed shortly after I had started to skew my time more heavily toward drilling and mindfulness training. As Dayne would have predicted, my confidence and skills quickly benefited, and I played with a sense of ease that I hadn't previously experienced. Despite continuing with my training, however, my good run eventually and unexpectedly ended. Right before the pendulum swung, I had texted Dayne and reported feeling surer of myself on the court, less vulnerable to swings in my play, and generally stronger in my game. As soon as the text left my phone, I felt a sense of dread that I had cursed myself—as if the mere act of acknowledging my confidence and improvement was beckoning the hand of hubris to smack me down. While my training had translated into more confidence, noticing my gains, and, heaven forbid, vocalizing them to my coach, made me feel attached to maintaining unvarying progress.

Around the same time as my ill-fated text, Dayne had started to post snippets of the book on social media, and I was receiving a steady flow of comments on the court noting my "seriousness" about pickleball. While no one cares much about anyone's game but their own, I was uncomfortable with the attention and internalized it as an unspoken edict that I had better be good given the work I was putting in. The higher my expectations crept, the tighter I became on the court. My flow reversed course and the ebb began.

Looking back, I had started turning every rec game into a searing referendum on my value as a player, as if my fate as a pickleball player would be sealed by my performance that day. The results always came back the same: "Should be performing better."

At this point in my long narrative, Dayne leapt in and said, "That's the problem! You think you are entitled to a result because of the work you put in!" I will spare you the details of the argument, but words were exchanged as I emphatically disagreed with the diagnosis. Entitlement wasn't the source of the problem, I argued. Equally unsavory character flaws—pridefulness, comparison, and impatience— were the villains of my story. I had been swimming in a sea of "shoulds"—where my mental game *should be* given my work with Dayne; what my physical game *should look like* given my diligent training; how I *should feel* about all the above.

Surrounded by athletic friends, I had been judging the cadence of my progress to be slower than it "*should be.*" That day at lunch, I hypothesized to Dayne that this particular ebb had come to a close when I could finally see the mental trap I had set for myself. **Once I recognized that I had unwittingly turned each game into a final exam for assessing my abilities, I could tear up the exam and let myself simply play each point, game, and**

match as just that—a moment in time with hopefully many more moments to come. I could scrap my imagined "acceptable" timeline of progression. Who cares if it takes me longer? I enjoy the grind and the process, so why rush it? Most importantly, it had become glaringly obvious that it was *far* past time to kick the imaginary peanut gallery out of my head and release myself from concern about anyone else's opinion of my abilities. Caring what other people thought of me had never done me any good off the court, and it certainly was not helping my cause on the court either.

Dayne then interjected, "Imagine how free you would be if you didn't care what anybody else thought of you?" I envisioned for a moment how my life might look different if I had sacked the chorus of imagined judgments years before. I certainly could have saved myself from some unnecessary suffering along the way. As I inched toward the mid-century mark, I had made steady progress putting less stock in other's judgments, but I realized I hadn't kicked the habit entirely.

By this time, our lunch meeting had ended, and it was time to head to the courts for a group clinic with Dayne. I was still unsure of how, or even whether, I could personally incorporate Dayne's confidence strategies, but I was game to try. For anyone who hasn't experienced a Dayne clinic, they are fast-paced, action-packed, and ill-suited for anyone whose mind is still out to lunch. With my thoughts still swirling from our conversation, my focus—and resultant play—were scattered and chaotic. Floundering during a clinic with Dayne was both uncomfortable and exactly what needed to happen.

Dayne had put so much time into me and my mental game that I didn't want to disappoint him by my inability to get my act together. I shuddered to think of being deemed an irremediable mental performance case. Unwittingly, I had given his imagined judgements a bullhorn and a front-row seat in my mind's chorus of critics. After that clinic, I kicked him out of the chorus, too, as I know he would want me to. To the extent he has opinions about my progress or lack thereof, that's fine, but they aren't my business, and they certainly don't get to influence my self-belief, for good or bad. **My confidence needs to be an inside job—a straight-up solo act.**

Since the clinic, I've mixed my own cocktail of practices and beliefs to try to create result-proof confidence. My recipe incorporates Dayne's original ingredients with a few tweaks to suit my palate. From Dayne's playbook, my training and preparation form the bedrock of my confidence and have reliably resuscitated my game when I'm ebbing more than flowing. Drilling until the dark cloud of a bad day passes continues to be the fastest way for me to get my feet back under me.

Not surprisingly, learning to release misses and drop into the next point has been the biggest uphill battle for me. Luckily, the pickleball gods have continued to dole out seemingly endless opportunities to practice letting go of errors. My biggest stumbling block to moving on from a mistake has been my own stubbornness. I don't *want* to let a mistake go; I *want to fix it* and make sure it doesn't happen again. While my tenacious dedication to problem-solving is beneficial in many arenas in my life, it's been a liability on the court, kidnapping my focus from the present and rerouting it to a backward-looking examination of what went wrong. Rather than releasing an error, the unwelcome squatters in my brain, Mr. Perfectionism and Mrs. No-Tolerance-for Errors, hop into action to identify the *cause* of the last error, as if the proper diagnosis will yield the remedy and prevent recurrence. Like I tell my children, there is a time and place for everything. Mid-game as the next ball is heading my way is neither the time nor the place for me to conduct an autopsy of my last error. Even as I have begun to recognize the counterproductive nature of my on-court, post-mortem examination of errors, learning to quiet my overthinking, problem-solving ways has been a beast of a habit to break.

While far from perfect, creating a post-miss ritual has helped me keep my eyes on the road ahead and out of the rearview mirror. Methodically forcing myself to enact the same ritual after an error helps me resist the strong tidal pull that mistakes exert on me toward the land of overthinking. For me, taking a full ribcage-expanding breath, relaxing my shoulders down my back, smiling at my partner, and repeating my chosen mantra helps redirect my mind back to the court and away from the paralysis-by-analysis sinkhole. There are still days when the devil on one shoulder snarls, "Don't mess up!" louder than the angel on the other whispers, "Now what?" But for the most part, I feel less tortured by errors and can refocus more quickly on the next point.

Finally, beyond my commitment to both training my physical shots and staying mentally present on the court, I revisit and repeat three interconnected decisions that I will keep making until they take root:

1. My progress is as it should be, regardless of what's happening around me.
2. My confidence isn't subject to any-one else's estimation of my abilities.
3. My confidence is unconditional.

Some days, I mix up the ingredients in the perfect ratio and get a glimpse into what Dayne means as *knowing* that I am untouchable. Other weeks, the best I can conjure up is a barely edible slurry and a commitment to keep faking it until I make it. More importantly, even on the bad days, I trust that I am slowly moving the needle toward resolute confidence, which is more than enough since perfection no longer gets to be my benchmark.

5

WELCOME THE MAKE-OR-BREAK MOMENTS

JILL

AS A FORMER ATTORNEY, I've spent more hours than I care to remember dissecting, massaging, and arguing about the definition of words. If you happen to read Supreme Court opinions to lull yourself to sleep, you know that monumental decisions have been based on disputed definitions of seemingly self-explanatory words. Years of combing over documents in search of words with the potential to absolve or incriminate has left me with a more-than-healthy respect for the power of the right combination of consonants and vowels.

While my obsession with words, their meaning, and usage feels predictable and par for the attorney course, I wouldn't have guessed that Dayne, as a coach and athlete, would share the same preoccupation. Arguably, he is even more of a word zealot than I am with a whole list of words that have been entirely blackballed from his vocabulary. Sometimes I wonder whether the smoke wafting from his neighborhood toward mine is coming from a bonfire fueled by pages ripped from his dictionary. Our reverence for words, however, arises from two different sources. Whereas I have always viewed words as weapons or shields to be used to protect or defend against another, Dayne respects words for their ability to shape our own thoughts. For Dayne, **the words we choose to describe our experiences on the court can alter not only our beliefs about ourselves, but also our potential**.

In an ideal world, our mutual respect for language would pave the road for seamless conversations about how to think about and articulate performance strategies. Just like Supreme Court justices have become logjammed by the definition of commonplace words, Dayne and I have locked horns about not only the meaning of words, but whether their mere utterance can breathe life into them.

This chapter, which delves into optimizing performance in the make-or-break moments, brought our word-off to a head. It was like the bad old days of debating the existence of a "slump." Just like *slump* is on Dayne's no-fly list, he has been staging a one-man boycott against the word *pressure* for years. He doesn't just dislike the word; he doesn't believe it exists, at least outside of what makes coal turn into diamonds. In his estimation, **"performance pressure" is as real as the boogeyman—a mental construct fueled only by our fears.** He rejects the idea that an athlete would be served by learning to "better manage" pressure; instead, he sees the make-or-break moments as **opportunities to be better**. Why, after all, would you allocate energy to getting better at tolerating a burden of your own creation rather than learning to transform moments of potential consequence into transformational opportunities?

In our first conversation about pressure—or not-pressure, as it were—the dissonance between my experience with the make-or-break moments and Dayne's ideas about how to thrive in them triggered my lawyerly instincts to poke holes in his assertions. It wasn't that I didn't believe what Dayne had to say about the illusion of pressure. I just wasn't convinced it was so illusory and susceptible to reframing for all people. What if some of us were missing the gene that converts high-stress moments into performance-enhancing opportunities rather than into a destabilizing force?

Dayne's passion for reframing the narrative about moments of potential consequence rivaled my doubt. "Anyone who spends enough time with me will get better in the big moments," he told me. Oh, to have that unapologetic confidence. If I could get *that*, I was willing to suspend my disbelief. It turns out that being a willing participant was the easy part. Learning to cut off the oxygen supply to the pressure boogeyman who had long ago set up camp in my mind has been a roller-coaster ride with stomach-clenching drops and cheer-inducing peaks. Many months later, I've become a repeat customer on the same ride, still learning to lean into the big moments rather than shrink away from them. Though I am still firmly in the "work-in-progress" phase, my hope is that my tumultuous experience embracing the make-or-break moments helps you lean into to the opportunities you may have been missing on the court.

DAYNE

From my earliest memories, coaches, sportscasters, and teammates associated the "pressure" of the make-or-break moments with negativity. Linked with adversity rather than opportunity, performance pressure was seen as a negative external force to be feared and "managed." The top athletes learned to tolerate and do their best when faced with this mental monster, while the less fortunate combusted under it. Like the psychological equivalent of the flu, the best outcome would be to minimize its debilitating symptoms.

That old-school coaching philosophy was based on the faulty assumption that high-stakes moments inevitably create performance-destabilizing "pressure."

How we choose to see the make-or-break moments will define the limits of our performance.

Ultimately, how we choose to see the make-or-break moments will define the limits of our performance. If we internalize the biggest moments as pressurized events to be *managed*, we unduly cap our performance ceiling at basic competence. Seeking to "tolerate pressure" is just a nice way of saying, "I hope I don't suck when it counts the most." Instead of thinking of pressure as something to deal with, we should put our arm around it and invite it into our every move. Rather than fearing or managing it, we need to reenvision the circumstances that create pressure as opportunities to reach new levels and become better.

What is pressure anyway? And does it deserve the bad rap it's been given? Many athletes express their experience of performing "under pressure" as if there were an *actual, external force acting upon them* rather than a *self-determined reaction to a moment of potential consequence*. Whereas a physical force like gravity is real and measurable, the "pressure" of match point is a pure creation of the mind. Despite how an athlete may experience it, the atmospheric pressure is no different during match point at the US Open than during a friendly rec game.

Pressure also isn't an emotion or physical reaction. It neither produces physical reactions in our bodies, nor fear, anxiety, doubt, and hesitation in our minds. Yet pressure has become synonymous with them all. This is not to deny the reality of the psychological and physical reactions that athletes experience in high-stakes moments. Those stress reactions are real and measurable, but pressure is just the fall guy; it never did anything to anyone! Our physical and psychological stress reactions aren't caused by *the pressure of the moment* but by *our perception of the moment*. Everything is neutral until we give it meaning. "Performance pressure" is just the term we have assigned to the decision to process moments of potential consequence as moments for potential failure. Do we go down the "what-if-I-mess-up" rabbit hole, or do we find the opportunity in the moment of stress? Don't blow it! Or now what?

> **Our physical and psychological stress reactions aren't caused by the pressure of the moment but by our perception of the moment.**

Make-It-Or-Break-It Moments

Pressure versus Opportunity

My group clinics offer a real-world lab for studying how athletes respond to small changes in competitive stress. Since the purpose of a clinic is to learn and improve, not to win, the level of stress "should" be low. My clinics aren't streamed on center court at Indian Wells, and no money is on the line. It doesn't matter that the stakes are low. Performance is highly sensitive, in *both* positive and negative ways, to barely perceptible changes in competitive stress.

As soon as I start to keep score in a simple drilling game, my students' performance shifts: Some players who are more technically proficient and don't miss a ball during noncompetitive drilling fall apart as soon as there is something to lose. Other players who stumbled through the noncompetitive parts of the clinic find the focus they previously lacked and play better. When the dial is turned up a bit more by playing a real game or by filming the play, the differences amplify: some players mystically play "above" their skill level; others plummet below it. Even though the weather, location, time of day, players, and skills practiced remain constant and only the level of competitive stress has changed, there is substantial variation in performance. **The sensitivity of performance**

to competitive stress underscores that our potential is dictated more by how we respond to intense moments than by our technical proficiency.

Just like some athletes are blessed with DNA that helps them jump higher and run faster, some competitors innately thrive in the make-or-break moments. The high stakes provide the oxygen these athletes need to reach max capacity. They don't talk about managing the big moments; they love and even crave them. That is a big clue to the pressure puzzle. An athlete's perception of the big moments, as moments to thrive or moments to be feared, will dictate their success.

On the flip side, some equally physically skilled athletes are dogged by a lower tolerance for stress from their earliest memories. Whether test-taking, public speaking, or match point, these athletes experience moments of potential consequence as anxiety-producing and disruptive to their performance. Rather than welcoming them in, they brace against them and fear "messing up" when it counts.

Since mindsets aren't fixed, even athletes who didn't come out of the womb chomping at the bit to play on center court *can* change their relationship with the big moments. Just as we can reframe our errors on the court as opportunities to galvanize our performance rather than debilitate it, we can also *choose* how we experience moments of potential consequence. Discomfort or fear is a habit like any other. With enough intention and repetition, *anyone* can develop a positive relationship with the make-or-break moments. There is no secret, overnight hack. It's a long game of purposeful habit replacement.

> Discomfort or fear is a habit like any other. With enough intention and repetition, anyone can develop a positive relationship with the make-or-break moments.

How to Transform Your Relationship with the Make-or-Break Moments

First, start by writing a list of the situations that place stress or pressure on your performance. The circumstances that create stress run the gamut and are unique to every athlete. For some athletes, tournaments or match point create peak stress, while for others the biggest source of anxiety is playing with or against specific players or being watched by a crowd.

Next, once you have identified the circumstances that increase your stress level on the court, ask yourself what you fear in those moments and situations. Be specific. The source of your stress doesn't hold any power; rather, it's the fear of the consequence of the make-or-break moment that disrupts performance. As diverse as the circumstances that cause competitive stress, if we distill the underlying fear down to its essence, we all generally fear (1) failing to meet our own expectations, or (2) failing to meet other's expectations. Those are powerful, core fears; it's no wonder they can wreak so much havoc on performance. That's why you've got to kick them out of the equation.

When our thoughts become hijacked by what-ifs on the court, our fears take us out of the present and catapult us into an anxious, fantasized future. Concentrating on the negative what-ifs is instinctive and habitual. It's a defense mechanism to protect us from the pain of failure based on the false belief that focusing on the catastrophe will help us avoid it. But the opposite is true. **When we see a moment as a chance to fail, our mindset becomes driven by the**

desire to avoid catastrophe, which only encourages it to manifest.

The answer isn't just to tell ourselves not to be fearful. Focusing on *not doing something* often just amplifies the power of the fear. Instead, **we have to give our mind a different, present-oriented focal point.** Rather than tethering our nervous system to an imagined catastrophic future, we need to help our mind out by throwing down an anchor into the present. Your anchor is the *opportunity* that exists in each moment of potential consequence.

Once you have figured out your stress triggers, it's time to identify the opportunities offered by those circumstances. Take your list of stressors and start switching out the language:

- *Replace* "I am afraid of embarrassing myself on center court" *with* "Playing on center court is an opportunity to integrate my hours of mental preparation and physical training."

- *Replace* "I am afraid of losing every match when I level up at a tournament" *with*

"Playing at a new level at a tournament is an opportunity to focus on the process and overcome my fear of losing."

The opportunity you choose will depend on your motivations and goals. **Whereas pressure opens the door to fear and passivity, opportunity ushers in confidence and conviction.**

Transform Competitive Stress into an Opportunity for Optimizing Performance

1. WHAT IS MY FEAR?

"I fear playing poorly at a tournament in front of my friends and family."

2. WHY DO I FEAR IT?

"I am afraid of embarassing myself. I am afraid of failing and disappointing myself."

3. WHAT IS THE OPPORTUNITY?

"Playing in front of my friends and family is an opportunity to play through my fear of failure, execute mental dominance, and integrate the time I have spent mentally preparing and physically training."

Even after years of coaching, I still slip into a fear mindset at times. During my first year as a Senior Pro, everything I had taught for years about using competitive stress to fuel performance was put to the test. At one tournament, while I was still trying to establish myself as one of the top players, my partner and I made it to the gold medal match, which was going to be live-streamed. We were scheduled to play in between the two pro men's semifinal matches, which meant there would be a packed house for our match.

Initially, the thought of playing our gold medal match in front of such a large crowd dramatically intensified my focus. As the first pro semifinal match was getting closer to finishing, something inside of me began to shift. Instead of the excited, focused athlete I was accustomed to being, my fearful brain started to take over my thoughts. I began ruminating about the possible negative what-if's: "What if I step on the live stream court as the favorite and play like garbage? All the work I've put in would be for nothing, and my credibility as a top senior pro and coach would instantly disappear. What if I embarrass myself in front of my students? Would they want to continue working with me? Would they think I was a fraud? What about my sponsors who have invested in my success? Would they want to drop me if my performance stunk up the court?"

The fear-driven thoughts looped in my mind as I waited to start our match. As soon as the winning pro team reached nine points, I headed to the bathroom for one last mental game prep work. I found an empty stall, walked in, locked the door, and just sat. Clothes still on, I closed my eyes and mentally revisited the hours of work I had put in leading up to this tournament. I saw the improvement, felt the growth, and knew I was ready. I made the conscious decision to shut down the what-if thought spiral that was corroding my confidence and transform the gold medal match into an opportunity to execute mental dominance, play through a fear of failure, and integrate the hours I had spent mentally preparing and physically training. Once I made the mental shift, I began to visualize the exact game plan we wanted to execute; I saw and felt perfection. The confidence I created overrode the negativity, leaving no room for what-ifs.

When I eventually stepped onto the court, my eyes glazed over and my peripheral vision shrunk, eliminating all outside distractions. As the referee called us to the net for his pre-match speech, I kept my eyes focused down onto the court and could barely hear a word he said. I started vibrating with a level of confidence difficult to describe. When I looked back up to acknowledge my opponents, I noticed one of them stared at me differently. He knew. He knew what the outcome of this match was going to be long before 0-0-2 was called.

As a younger athlete, the what-ifs and fear of losing stymied me from playing to my potential and stopped me from pursuing opportunities in which I couldn't guarantee success. Since a fear-based response to moments of consequence is a **habit of the mind** and **not a fixed condition**, I created new habits and trained myself through repetition and practice to focus on the opportunity rather than possible future calamity.

To create a new habitual response to competitive stress, as oversimplified as it may sound, we first need to change the way we talk about and therefore *think about* the big moments. **Begin by committing to a global "find and replace" in your vocabulary that substitutes *pressure* with *opportunity*.** Then, the hard work of practice and massive repetition begins.

A habit is something we cement into our unconscious by repeating it over and over. That means we can create new habits in the same way. The challenge is taking the necessary action to repeat the good habits over and over.

Welcome in the conditions that challenge you on the court, and practice tapping into the opportunities offered by the hard moments over and over again. Get comfortable with the discomfort, and accept it as part of the process. When you feel the butterflies, remember that the goal isn't to eliminate the intensity you feel in the big moments. That is as foolish as trying to solve a low tolerance for errors by eliminating mistakes. It's impossible and counterproductive. The butterflies are just a tell that there is a sliding door in front of you. On one side resides the fear of failure; on the other lives the opportunity to optimize your performance. Even catching yourself in the act of casting your gaze into a future of negative outcomes gives you the chance to

> The butterflies are just a tell that there is a sliding door in front of you. On one side resides the fear of failure; on the other lives the opportunity to optimize your performance.

reroute your attention to a specific present intention. Eventually, rather than bracing against moments of potential consequence as events to survive, with enough practice, you will begin to step into them with greater focus, confidence, and a sense of calm.

JILL

Before pickleball, I had little experience in competitive sports. The high-water mark of my adolescent athletic career was competing on my high school's very first soccer team, which boasted a record of one win per season. Remembering my shin guards was the most "pressurized" moment offered by my soccer experience. As an adult, I turned my attention to more solitary endurance sports, like triathlons and long-distance running. Though I competed often, I disclaimed any interest in reaching the podium, or even my place in the pack. Framing races as an accountability tool for my training, I set my aspirations so low that mere survival ensured success. Even so, as race day drew near, rather than greeting the chance to compete with excitement, dread would start to descend upon me. The night before each race, I'd gravely warn my husband, "I don't think I'll be able to finish tomorrow." He'd politely pretend we didn't have this conversation before every race and remind me why I was more than prepared enough. As if reading from a preordained script, I'd wrap up our Groundhog Day conversation with musings that I could always crawl my way to the finish line if worst came to worst, but assuming I survived, I was hanging up my racing belt for good.

My training partners were polar opposite to me; both former collegiate athletes, they were natural, experienced competitors. While training, our relative differences were negligible, but when the starting gun fired, they were like cheetahs who had just spied a gazelle while I felt like a fluffy, lop-eared bunny whose heart might explode from the sudden loud noise. They seemed to be equipped with a hidden gear that kicked in during races that let them leave everything out there. I'd run the races as if I had been hired as a professional pacer—steady, consistent, never surpassing third gear. While I was flooded with relief as I crossed the finish line, moments later, the relief was replaced with disappointment that I had overprioritized merely finishing and had left enough fuel in the tank to run the race again.

By the time I made my way to the pickleball court, I had racked up decades of unconsciously focusing my attention on fending off failure instead of maximizing my abilities. Just as I often realized at the finish line of a race that I had run too safely to guarantee I'd finish, I shied away from opportunities if I couldn't ensure meeting my own expectations or others' imagined ones. As limiting as my fear of failure could be, it made me dogged in my focus and preparation. If I had enough anxiety coursing through my veins, my drive to ensure no stone was left unturned was unbeatable. While I could see the benefit of my anxiety-fueled work ethic, I was often blinded to how my fear-based mentality could negatively affect my ability to perform.

The nature of pickleball threw a wrench in my system and challenged my tacit assumption that my fear-based mindset was helpful rather than undermining. At tournaments, I quickly learned that approaching moments of potential consequence on the pickleball court from a place of fear was not only ineffectual but counterproductive. Just as I had entered exams and legal battles bracing myself for the worst, I played tournaments with a pit in my stomach that was flavored more by dread than by butterflies. Whereas my fear-the-worst mentality helped me get laser-focused when it counted academically or professionally, it completely backfired on the court. Instead of providing me an anxiety-fueled edge as it had in other arenas, the extra adrenaline often exited my body in a baffling interplay of tightness and freneticism on the court.

Rather than seeing my fear-based motivational style as a way of driving my hard work, I began to see how corrosive and self-limiting it was. Beyond disrupting my performance, my tournament nerves often took the fun out of competing as well. Acquiescing to a lower ceiling of performance was one thing, but giving up on enjoying the moment was entirely unacceptable. Like a pictogram that rearranged the pixels to reveal a complete image, I could finally see the cost of importing my well-worn, suffer-fest approach onto the pickleball court: I wasn't just depriving myself of the ability to play better in the big moments; my way threatened to drain the joy right out of pickleball. Bringing the same fear-based habits on the pickleball court that had kept me successful but unhappy in my career for too long would be such a wasted opportunity. Rather than battening down the hatches to keep out moments of potential consequence, I realized it was finally time to try what Dayne had been pushing me to do all along and blow the doors open.

I came up with a list of the conditions that placed stress on my game. The circumstances that I internalized as pressure were all related to the "who" rather than the "where, when, what, or how." While match point didn't elevate my blood pressure much anymore, playing against a friend in a tournament felt like being pulled apart by a medieval stretching device. Even partnering *with* a good friend could get me spinning out of fear of disappointing my friend *and* partner.

Logically, I knew that as friends on the court, whether as partners or opponents, we all agreed to the same set of rules: we were there to win, and it wasn't a violation of a friend code to be a competitor. Despite intellectually understanding the tacit contract of competition, my brain and heart struggled to get on the same page. When competing with and against friends, there was a chronic tug-of-war between two sets of rules: Do I show up as a competitor, or do I should up as a friend? When I see my friend/opponent is frustrated and struggling, do I continue to go after her as the player who is breaking the way I would with an unknown competitor? Or do I give her breathing room to recover as I would for a friend and let down my partner? I couldn't see at the time that the two sets of rules I had constructed weren't mutually exclusive or contradictory. Trying to pick the right rule to follow at the right moment had set me up to fail as either a competitor and partner or as a friend.

While I could quickly identify the circumstances that created stress for me on the court, initially, my mind flatlined when tasked with finding the opportunity in those moments. My poor unwitting partners and I hopped on several wild rides of trial and error as I tried on different "opportunities." Eventually, I learned that I needed to *lean into* the chance to overcome my fear of competing with and against friends and to accept that I may not show up perfectly every time. Most of my pickleball friends had deeper competitive, athletic backgrounds and had developed the emotional muscles to effectively toggle between the modes of friend and competitor long ago. I committed to re-envisioning competing with and against friends as an opportunity to grow that muscle, knowing that imperfection would be guaranteed along the way.

Instead of fixating on my fear of getting it wrong, I assigned myself the task of mentally blurring out the people across the net from me and focusing on the patterns of play, which helped me switch mental tracks from fear to problem-solving. Instead of focusing on the "who" of the other team, I gave myself the job of figuring out what was and wasn't working against the two players across the net.

Next, it was time to practice. Luckily for me, putting myself repeatedly in uncomfortable positions is right up my suffer-loving alley. I sought out games with and against the people who most elevated my heart rate. Sometimes my strategies worked; other times I had to use all my might to pick my bruised ego off the court and dust it off. I felt myself making steady progress and gaining confidence in my ability to leverage circumstances that had previously thrown me for a loop. Amid seeking out increasingly uncomfortable opportunities, I agreed to play in a local tournament with and against many of my closest friends. Though just a small local match that didn't even cost a dime, the relational stress I felt was more intense than any tournament I had played to date.

The very best thing happened: everything went wrong. My overactive brain was running interference with my body, and I felt as if my new mental performance strategies were leaving me high and dry. I couldn't serve the ball into the big blue square across the net from me to save a life. It was the strangest sensation to have my right forearm completely disobey what I was telling it to do. As I served out-ball after out-ball, rather than getting frustrated with me, my small but mighty partner paddle-tapped me, made me laugh, and kept moving forward. At moments, she essentially threw me on her five-foot-four frame like a very tall, lanky backpack and carried us across the finish line.

I texted Dayne in the middle of matches lamenting my service issue and how deeply uncomfortable the whole experience felt. He tossed me a text lifeline with the exact words that I needed to hear to pull myself out of my mental puddle. He put an end to my pity party and reframed what had felt like a complete mental toughness failure. He reminded me that despite my service issue, we didn't break individually or as a partnership. Rather than obsessing about the liability of my serve, he helped me see that the embarrassment I was feeling was just a disguised opportunity to dig deeper and stay tough despite what I couldn't control, which, at least temporarily, was my serve. My serves started limping their way into the right square, and we somehow fought our way to win all our matches that day.

I'm not going to say I enjoyed that day. I didn't like it one bit. But surviving a pickleball implosion was the reminder I needed that challenging moments, even when they don't turn out as you'd like, are not only survivable, but where a lot of magic can happen. In many ways, my worst fears on the court had coalesced. I could not hit the simplest shot in pickleball and was on track to singlehandedly lose our matches despite my partner's best efforts. The support from my partner, friends, and coach when I wasn't crushing it and finding a way to tap into the extra gear that had been so elusive to me was a far better gift than killing it in that moment.

Much like the other mental performance skills I've worked on with Dayne, since that local tournament, I've made progress, backslid, put back on my big-girl pants, and flung myself back into the make-or-break moments. My practice "inviting in" moments of potential consequence on the court has carried over off the court, and I keep finding myself saying yes to real-life opportunities that had previously felt too scary. I've also felt increasingly fortified in some of the seemingly crazy choices I've made over the last year, like leaving a stable job and writing a book about pickleball.

The key to transforming my relationship with make-or-break moments was being brave enough to see the opportunities, invite them in, and be willing to eat dirt sometimes, knowing that no amount of public failure was as bad as avoiding opportunities for success. If your experience is anything like mine, you'll know you've hit the jackpot growth opportunity if you find yourself swearing like a sailor and wondering whether you can possibly change what feels like a fixed trait about yourself. When you hit that

> **The key to transforming my relationship with make-or-break moments was being brave enough to see the opportunities, invite them in, and be willing to eat dirt sometimes, knowing that no amount of public failure was as bad as avoiding opportunities for success.**

inflection point, the stickiest of stuck places, take the biggest breath you can and get back to work, reminding yourself that your imagined limitations only have the power that you give them. Finally, if all else fails and you become tempted to hoist up the white flag of defeat, find a partner, friend, or coach who is immune to your very persuasive arguments about your own shortcomings and can help you see your potentiality and progress when you can't.

6

FIND AND BECOME A GREAT PARTNER

DAYNE

EARLY IN MY SENIOR pro career, I received a text from my mixed doubles partner informing me she wouldn't be able to play in an upcoming tournament. I immediately texted Jen Dawson, who is one of, if not the best, senior female pro player of all time. I had wanted to play with her for a long time, but she was always booked. I knew my text would be a long shot. I excitedly hit *Send* and then stared at my phone, anxiously awaiting her response. I eventually had to chastise myself for my overeagerness: "Dude, calm down. You're fifty years old, acting as if you're waiting for your seventh-grade crush to agree to be your date for the Valentine's Day dance." Finally, later that evening, she texted back, saying she was free and would love to play with me. I may or may not have broken out into a happy dance.

At the tournament, we cruised through our first round but then hit a very strong team in the second. We lost the first game, clawed our way through the second, barely winning it, and then found ourselves down 6-10 in the third. As our opponents got ready to serve at 10-6-1, I thought to myself, "Welp, this is where we find out what we're made of."

I knew I wasn't going to quit and assumed Jen wouldn't either, but there was no way of knowing how we'd respond as a team. I called our last time-out and gave Jen two fist bumps, which eventually turned into our time-out ritual. During the sixty-second break, we didn't say much, but I paid attention to her body language and the look in her eyes. She looked *fearless*. That singular moment helped grow my own confidence because I *saw* that she believed the match was not nearly over.

At 10-6-1, we had a long-fought point, defending their attacks and getting stuck in transition for multiple resets and lobs, but we somehow found our way back to the kitchen, neutralizing their offense. After what seemed like 100 more dinks, we won that point and lived to return at 6-10-2. We won that point quickly, which gave us the ball back and new life. Even though we were still down big, it felt different. We took two quick points to get us to 8-10-1, forcing our opponents to call their last time-out. I gave Jen the two-fist bump ritual, and we calmly walked back to our water bottles and towels. Again, not much was said, but our energy spoke volumes; we knew this match was ours. Our chemistry totally connected.

We won that match and eventually won the entire tournament. We've gone on to have a very strong partnership, winning Nationals, the US Open, and multiple other tournaments along the way. It was that single moment for me, down 6-10, where our chemistry aligned, and I knew that our partnership was one that amplified each other's confidence and performance. I've always said publicly that Jen Dawson has been my favorite partner, male or female, not because of her talent, but because of how easy and seamless our connection has always been.

Finding and cultivating a connected and successful partnership like the one that I've been fortunate enough to have with Jen can be one of the biggest challenges in pickleball. As most of us have experienced, when partners are synced up, the whole is stronger than the individual parts. The converse, however, is equally true: Rather than upleveling one another, partners can drag each other down below even the lowest common denominator. This chapter dives into strategies on how to find compatible partners and maximize your partnership's ability to elevate each other's performance.

1. Finding a Synergistic Partnership

Until now, we've only focused on how to optimize our *individual* mental performance. Other people's emotions, thoughts, and judgments have only concerned us so far as developing strategies to keep their energetic output from infecting our performance. However, unless you only play singles, mental performance doesn't operate in a vacuum. On the tiny pickleball court, our partner's mind is just steps away, either connecting, disengaging, or clashing with our own. The resulting synergy or dissonance with our partner dictates the magic or mayhem that follows. A synergistic partnership requires both *tangible* compatible skill sets and *intangible* partnership chemistry. We'll start by digging into the nitty-gritty of identifying the tangible skills required for a successful partnership and then explore how to assess partnership chemistry.

A. The Tangibles: Compatible Skills Sets

Just like love is a necessary but insufficient ingredient for marriages that weather the test of time, partnerships require more than just chemistry to thrive under competitive stress. In the strongest partnerships, each partner possesses hard skills that complement one another. When we find the right partner, it feels like two

> **Partnerships require more than just chemistry to thrive under competitive stress.**

adjoining puzzle pieces clicking into place. Just like you wouldn't try to find a matching puzzle piece without knowing the contours of the piece in your hand, you can't know what to look for in a partner until you are familiar with your own ridges, curves, and grooves. Otherwise, you'll be blindly fishing in a heaping mound of pieces, distracted by the pieces that look the best on their own but won't fit with yours.

Consequently, the partnership process begins with an **honest self-inventory**, examining how you prepare, play, and communicate, and what your goals are. To start, ask yourself the following questions:

Finding the Right Player
Step 1: Who Are You As a Player?

PICKLEBALL SELF-INVENTORY QUESTIONNAIRE
1. **How do I prepare and train?**
2. **What is my playing style?** (i.e. Aggressive/Risk-Taking v. Patient/Grinding)
3. **What are my strengths and weaknesses?**
4. **What are my communication preferences?**
5. **What are my goals?**

Doing a self-inventory can be daunting. Often, we don't have clarity or objectivity on our own strengths and weaknesses. If you get stuck, seek input from your coach or other trusted players. Or use your smartphone to get smarter by videotaping yourself while you drill and play. It may not be easy to watch yourself at first, but it will teach you as much or more about yourself as a player than even the best coach.

Once you understand yourself as a player, start considering the attributes that would best compliment your skill set. You and your partner don't have to have the same or even similar player DNA. **The only thing that matters is that your skill sets are compatible, which can be born of similarity or difference.**

The workable permutations of pairings are unlimited: Some aggressive players need a yin to their yang, while others thrive with fellow risk-takers. One chatterbox may jive with another talker, while others may not be able to share the airtime. Some strategists need a like-minded tactician, while others are balanced out well by a see-ball-hit-ball type. Because there are no hard-and-fast rules for player compatibility, the best way to figure out the formula that works for you is to test the waters with a diverse pool of players and start observing.

Finding the Right Partner
Step 2: Is a Player a Compatible Partner?

PARTNERSHIP COMPATIBILITY QUESTIONNAIRE
1. Does my partner's way of preparing and training align with mine? Does it matter to me?
2. Does her playing style meld with mine?
3. Does she have the hard or soft skill I can't live without?
4. Does her way of communicating make me bulletproof or do I have to tune her out?
5. Does she share similar goals? Does it matter to me?

At this point in my career, I know the **must haves, may haves**, and **can't haves** in my partners. Everyone's rubric will look different, but here's the general formula that works for me: My very first consideration is a player's mental toughness. Shocking, right? I will take a strong mental game over the best court skills every day of the week because without the former, the latter will fall flat under stress. Next, I'll look at playing style. As someone with a very aggressive playing style, I can pair well with either fellow aggressors or grinders, but fast hands have to be a part of the package. After playing style, I consider game IQ, including a player's understanding of the game and willingness to engage in strategic discussions. With the rapid momentum swings in pickleball, the ability to pivot on a dime during the make-or-break moments is vital. Making the necessary adjustments may require one or both of us to shelve our egos, switch preferred roles on the court, and craft a new strategy in complete departure from our original plan. If we as a partnership can't flex, bend, and evolve together in response to new information in real time under stress, we will not ultimately succeed and have no business on the court together. Finally, I will not partner with a quitter. We might lose, but no matter what happens, I need to know that we don't break and we don't quit. If I feel the quit in a partner before the final score is called, we won't partner again.

As you learn your own game better, you'll figure out where you can be flexible and where there is only one right answer. Keep track of your own list of must haves, may haves, and can't halves:

Finding the Right Partner
Partner Compatibility Survey

Partner "Must Haves"	(i.e. "fast hands")
Partner "May Haves"	(i.e. "similar goals")
Partner "Can't Haves"	(i.e. "negative communication style")

Know that as soon as you've cracked the code, your game may progress, and your original prerequisites for partnership may change. The key, however, is to be your own keenest spectator, statistician, and notetaker and develop the discernment skills that allow you to respond to the evolving information your games continue to offer.

B. The Intangibles: Partnership Chemistry

Now for the bad news for the planners and control freaks among us. The best notes, spreadsheets, analysis, and even rec play can't predict two of the most important components of a partnership: tournament partner chemistry and connection under competitive stress.

Partnership chemistry is no different than the energetic connection that makes some relationships click and others fizzle. It's like the date set up by your friends with the "perfect match" for you. You share more similarities than differences, but somehow your competing electrons and protons create an energetic vacuum rather than electricity. The same is true on the court; finding a partner who is perfect on paper is no guarantee that you'll sync up as partners. Unfortunately, whereas hard skills can be improved, chemistry can't be taught. You either have it or you don't. If you don't, cut your losses and move on.

Chemistry off the court and in rec play is a good start but doesn't tell the whole story. A partnership's ability to remain connected during the make-or-break moments is impossible to predict outside of a tournament environment. Your first tournament together is a fertile testing ground for your partnership. Use it together wisely; when you get home, assess how your partnership performed under competitive stress:

Finding the Right Partner
Step 3: How Did Our Partnership Perform Under Competitive Stress

TOURNAMENT PARTNERSHIP QUESTIONNAIRE
1. What happened to our partnership in the make-or-break moments?
2. Did our connection falter when we were down?
3. Under stress, did my partner go into panic mode and get too fired up or not fired up enough?
4. Was my partner excited to get back on the court after a loss? Was my partner excited to keep rolling after a win?
5. Could we talk strategy and adjustments when things were going sideways?

Tournaments are adrenaline-rich environments. Connected partnerships are energized by the invisible high-frequency current running through the courts, while fragile partnerships get fractured by it. Even if you have the same goals, training priorities, and playing styles, if you can't stay connected during the biggest moments, it's time to move on.

2. Being a Good Partner

While finding the right partner involves some guess-work, strategy, and luck, being a good partner is entirely within your control. It's all relationship 101 stuff, but it's also easier said than done, especially under competitive stress. Most of you will read these recommendations and believe that you already do them. From watching a lot of pickleball, I beg to differ. Virtually all of us, including me and Jill, could improve on one, if not multiple, fronts because (1) we are human, and (2) it's incredibly difficult to consistently self-regulate over the course of a long, tiring tournament day.

If you want the Reader's Digest version, being a good partner can be summed up in a few words: don't be a jerk. Since these kindergarten essentials often elude even the best of us on the court, let's break down the why and how of good partner citizenship skills.

Your connection with your partner is your most valuable currency. It's more essential to your success than your unreturnable forehand pancake or her killer two-handed backhand.

Your connection with your partner is your most valuable currency. It's more essential to your success than your unreturnable forehand pancake or her killer two-handed backhand. That means your most important job is to protect that connection like your life depends on it. No matter how strong your partnership, you've got to treat that connection like a spring chick. Neglect it, squeeze it too hard, or feed it bad seed and that puff of fluff is a goner.

Partnership chemistry in pickleball is a vulnerable commodity for a couple of reasons. The size of the court keeps you so physically close to one another that your partner *will* feel your energy. If you say, "No worries!" but your body is screaming, "You suck!" your partner will see and feel it. Additionally, the speed of the game and rapid scoring runs require successful partnerships to stay in perpetual communication and make multiple micro-adjustments on a second-by-second basis. The amount of real-time pivoting required in a game, particularly when things are going south, is a Pandora's box of frustration and finger-pointing waiting to be sprung. How do you make sure not to squash your baby chick? Be positive, find the method that works in your partnership to stay connected throughout a game, and eliminate blame from your vocabulary. I warned you. It's not rocket science, but it's decidedly not easy.

C. Remaining Positive and Connected

The number-one partnership killer is negativity and separation on the court. Getting negative encompasses far more than your words. Most players don't verbally berate their partners; their body is their tell. If you think no one else is picking up on your negative energy, sagged shoulders, eye rolls, or frustrated grimace, I promise you at least three people are: the one standing next to you and the two across the net from you. The one next to you received the "you suck" message loud and clear and now is dedicating energy either to "not missing again" or getting you out of her head. Either option lands you farther from the podium. As soon as your partnership visibly broke, those two players across the net set the table, tucked a napkin into their shirts, and got ready to eat you for lunch.

Controlling your body language and energy in the heat of the battle is incredibly challenging, but it's one of your most important jobs. Creating a simple routine to reconnect after a miss is a good place to start. After your partner makes an error, if you get the slightest inkling of an emotional dip, your priority is to paddle tap, de-emphasize the miss, solidify your connection, and guide your collective focus to the next shot.

After your partner makes an error, if you get the slightest inkling of an emotional dip, your priority is to paddle tap, de-emphasize the miss, solidify your connection, and guide your collective focus to the next shot.

The underlying message is simple: "You're good. I'm good. We're good. Next point." It doesn't have to be lots of words or a heartfelt soliloquy, just a simple, positive redirect. The cost benefit analysis is a no-brainer: nothing can go wrong by giving your partner positivity after a miss. If you neglect the opportunity to boost up your partner and she goes down the toilet bowl, you've got a lot more work to do to fish her back out.

D. Banish Blame

Teams win and lose together. There is no I miss/you miss. We miss, we make, we lose, and we win. Sure, your partner may have an off day and make more mistakes, but the second you let yourself off the hook by pointing the finger, you're toast. I don't just mean in the match. This includes publicly blaming your partner after a loss. As soon as you indulge in the blame game, you've set into effect a negative chain reaction for you, your current partnership, and any future partners who get wind that you're *that* type of partner. Banning blame from your vocabulary is the only way to grow as a player and, you know, be a decent human.

Eliminating blame doesn't mean avoiding conversations about adjustments. You can stay out of the blame zone by approaching adjustments from a "we" rather than a "you" perspective. If your partner is being targeted or keeps missing a certain shot, they already know it. Pointing it out during your time-out is counterproductive. Instead, come up with a strategy that takes some heat off your partner or changes things up for a few points. After the game, there is still zero value in finger-pointing. Not to your partner, not to your coach, not to your opponents, not even to your spouse. There is no spousal privilege exception here! Just the thought, even unarticulated, is a barrier to your own growth and improvement. **Your post-game analysis should focus on your controllables, which start and end with you.**

How to Be a Great Partner

1. **Stay positive, regardless of the score.**

2. **Create a ritual to reconnect in between every point.**

3. **Eliminate blame. Win and lose together as a team.**

3. Communicating Before the Big Day

We'll talk about the pre-tourney convo in more detail in chapter 7 when we do a deep dive into tournament preparation. But for now, we'll cover how to connect with your partner pre-tournament. The content and depth of a pre-tournament conversation will heavily depend on each partnership's communication style. At a minimum, discuss the general strategy you'll use to start each match and the adjustments you will make if the original game plan isn't working. If you know the opponents you'll be facing, your strategy can be more detailed based on their strengths and vulnerabilities.

Determine how you want to respond stylistically in the most challenging moments. For example, I talk about staying aggressive in the make-or-break moments, continuing to initiate, and playing our pace. For a partnership of grinders, the conversation may be about slowing down the game and forcing an error. Wherever you land stylistically, recommit to staying positive, connected, and unbreakable in the big moments.

4. Determining When to Break Up a Partnership and When to Keep Working

When a partnership hits a rough patch, it can be difficult to decide whether to keep working through the kinks or seek greener pastures. The decision of when to call it quits depends on so many variables that it can be hard to generalize. Assuming you aren't married to or best friends with your partner, here are a few goal-posts to consider:

The obvious data to mine is your tournament record. More losses than wins aren't necessarily the death knell of a partnership, but if you are racking up more Ls than Ws, you do need to look at the "quality" of your losses. If you are new partners, your first tournament likely won't provide enough data unless you identify that you don't have chemistry, in which case it's never too early to cut bait. Tournaments two and three should give you enough information to know if you're getting better together, even if your record doesn't reflect it yet.

It's worth repeating: film your matches. There is a lot going on during a tournament, which can make it hard to assess the quality of a loss or win. Watching film will give you far more insight than your real-time perceptions.

If you have more serious goals, you may give your partnership a shorter runway to assess its viability. For most amateurs, if you enjoy playing together and find that love for one another on the court, you'll have far greater bandwidth to tolerate the ups and downs of tournament play before calling it quits.

When to End a Partnership

> ☑ You have poor partnership chemistry.
>
> ☑ You don't enjoy playing with one another anymore.
>
> ☑ Your tournament record and the quality of your wins and losses reflect a lack of progress as a team.

Finally, remember the rule of the common denominator. If you're burning through partners as fast as pickleballs crack on a cold day, it's time to redirect the spotlight back on yourself and figure out what part you're playing in the partnership puzzle. Think of it this way: if you can't identify an area where you could improve as a partner, I promise you aren't looking hard enough. While partnering is a two-way street, each of our jobs is to consistently engage in honest self-assessment and commit to cleaning up our side of the street so that ultimately the roadway is cleared for chemistry to work its magic.

JILL

1. Finding My Partner(s)

Solving the partnership puzzle has been surprisingly challenging, uncomfortable, and eye-opening for me. As a generally self-aware person, I was surprised how clueless I was about myself as a player and a partner. It was only in writing this chapter that I started to develop a clearer picture of how I show up on the court and what that means for both partnering decisions and the work I have left to do to be a better partner.

Until recently, I'd have told you that I could partner with just about anyone. As a result, I did. When asked to play in a tournament or competitive local event, I said yes before the question was finished. After many tournaments with just as many partners, I've gathered lots of data to disprove my original hypothesis.

Why was I so off the mark in my estimation of myself as an endlessly flexible partner? Without knowing much about pickleball or myself as a competitive athlete, I incorrectly assumed that my off-court strengths would be predictive of my on-court skills. In my everyday life, I like and get along with just about anyone. I mistook my ability to connect *off-court* with most people as a proxy for my ability to connect *on-court* with them. As a result, I've partnered with a lot of people because I assumed that enjoying their company would automatically translate into playing well together. I quickly learned that I woefully underestimated the complexity of partnerships and that liking one another, at least for me, is an insufficient basis for a successful partnership.

I also underestimated how my sensitive nature would impact my partnership decisions. For good and for bad, I'm a sensitive person and an empath. These qualities make me a good friend and emotional detective (if there were such a thing). Left unchecked and paired with the wrong partner, my super-sensors are a huge liability on the pickleball court. While a more strategic player could recall the sequence of shots at the conclusion of a game, in my early days on the court, I could have recited a play by play of all the feelings whizzing across the net. When I sensed my partner, or even my opponent, was upset, my attention and energy drifted from the point in progress to their distress, which was helpful to exactly no one.

Despite the indisputable challenges my sensitivity creates on the court, Dayne never wavered in his position that it is an essential, immutable part of me that I need to learn to manage, rather than quash, in a competitive environment. The strategies that I have acquired to wrangle my wandering-empath's eye have ended up informing my personal list of "partnership-must haves/can't haves/and may haves."

The top of my partnership-must-have list is having a compatible communication style. I need to communicate. A lot. To keep my mind from drift-ing, I need to call virtually every ball, resulting in a cacophony of "mine" and "yours" that makes my side of the court sound as if a very tall coxswain lost her rowing crew and stumbled onto the pickleball court. It's a hack that keeps my busybody brain appropriately engaged even when the ball isn't coming my way. A player who needs quiet to focus would want to ship me and my constant burble to the Thames. On the flip side, my partners with complementary communication styles thrive on the interaction and remind me to keep talking when my attention starts to fizzle.

My "partnership-can't-have" list is also rooted in communication style. Negativity, in all its iterations, is a hard pass for me. Beyond my preference for not being miserable on the court, I always want to bring my best and my best runs for the hills in response to the silent treatment, exasperated sighs, or overt criticism. One of my superpowers is reading people. I can tell someone's mood before they open their mouth or raise an eyebrow. That helps me read my opponents, but it also means I can *feel* my partner's frustration or disappointment even if they are telling me through gritted teeth, "No worries." Previously, no matter how depleting I found a partner's communication style or energetic presence on court, I saw it as my work to better tolerate and accommodate it. Those days are over. Since no one pays me to play pickleball, I've decided that type of work is far beyond my nonexistent paygrade.

I partner best with even-keeled, positive players who are nonplussed by errors. One of my favorite partners finds the most improbable way of apologizing for my mistakes. If I pop up a ball that results in an unreturnable put-away, she'll say with complete sincerity, "I'm sorry. I should be able to get that." I suppose if she dove across the concrete, breaking various limbs in the process, she could have rectified my error. So yes, her bad. While taking ownership for my errors is completely unnecessary and often comical, her underlying message is clear and anxiety-reducing: the misses and makes are ours.

As much as positivity and compatible communication styles are non-negotiables for me, my list of "may-haves" or "don't-have-to-haves" is far more comprehensive. Sure, I play better with certain playing styles and strengths, but I am not wed to them. It's nice to have similar goals and training regimens, but I don't much care about that either. If I connect well with a partner and feel comfortable with them, I can adapt to almost anything else.

When my son was entering kindergarten, I remember the principal explaining the importance of creating a positive learning environment where children felt at ease and happy. Research showed, he explained, that children who are happy at school learn better, are better behaved, and demonstrate more emotional literacy. More than having the top facilities or the best curriculum, children thrive when they are at ease. I am a lot like a kindergartener: It doesn't matter if I have the partner with the best skills. If I am not happy and comfortable, I can't perform well, and it's much harder for me to behave well too! I've had the partner with the best hard skills on the court, but I proved time and again that, when coupled with negativity, I will underperform every time. It took massive amounts of trial and error, but now that I've figured out my list of non-negotiables, it's easy to pass over the shiny pennies and find partnerships where we can elevate one another's performance.

2. Becoming a Better Partner

Since beginning to think more intentionally about partnerships, I've become, at least I hope, a better partner. I've learned to better titrate the amount of strategic information to discuss with any given partner. While a game plan is often helpful for me, some of my partners are more instinctual players and discussing strategy is counterproductive. Deciding how much, when, and what to say previously felt like a dance where I could cripple my partner by stepping on her foot with a stiletto heel at any moment. I've gotten better at asking partners what works for them and making adjustments when I see a partner go into information overload. I also realized that while I like having a spot or two to target or avoid, or a general strategy, too much information delivered between points trips me up and gets me thinking too much and not playing enough. Now that I know that about myself, I let my partners know the type and timing of information that helps and hinders me.

The biggest evolution in my partnership skills came from shifting my perspective from *me* to *we*. Once I started to view both my mental and physical performance as *one half of two interlocking parts*, I was able to quiet my ego, stop obsessing over my own performance and shortcomings, and start thinking about how I can best support my partner. While writing this chapter, I was preparing to play in a tournament in which I'd face off against some teams I particularly wanted to beat. The night before the tournament, my ego kicked into full gear and clouded my head with unhelpful *I don't want to lose to X* thoughts. I shared my ego-driven ruminations with a friend, who acknowledged that that line of thinking would pull me down the drain and urged me to pick a different focal spot for my busy brain.

Fortunately, partnership dynamics were front and center in my mind. I realized that my self-focused fears had left my partner off the court altogether. As soon as I shifted my focus away from a self-interested outcome to our partnership and my duty to bring my half of our interlocking whole, my body and mind relaxed. On the court, maintaining a strong connection to my partner kept my mind out of the ego-gutter and allowed me to find my game and enjoy myself, even during the games I had most dreaded.

My work to become a better partner is far from over. Like almost all the skills I've learned on the court, as soon as I think I've nailed a skill, new challenges arise that make me realize I still have a lifetime of improvement ahead of me. Being a human being is complicated enough, so it shouldn't come as a surprise how challenging it can be to synchronize two human beings in a competitive environment. Though not always easy and sometimes downright painful, learning to be a better partner has paid dividends far beyond the court. Finding better ways to communicate under stress, showing up as a *we* rather than a *me* even when the chips are down, and finding joy amidst the chaos has been one of the most fulfilling parts of my pickleball journey, both on and off the court.

7

MAXIMIZE YOUR TOURNAMENT PERFORMANCE

DAYNE

IN 2021, WHEN THE Minto US Open Pickleball Championships announced it would hold a split age event,[1] I reached out to the best player in the game, Ben Johns, not thinking he'd agree to play with me. He surprised me with a yes, which was simultaneously mind-blowing and terrifying. If we lost, I'd be the one to blame; if we won, he'd get all the credit. This was the truest definition of lose/lose for me.

While I knew Ben didn't give our event one millisecond of attention as he prepared for the US Open, it was all I focused on during my training sessions. I had to learn not only how to play the right side, but also how do it in a smaller space than I was used to. "Dink and defend" is how I prepared and all I told myself during practice. Knowing the other pro player would be straight ahead of me in each match up, if I couldn't defend their attacks, we were going to be in big trouble.

Every night from 11:00 p.m. to 2:00 a.m., I studied video on how Collin Johns played his right-side role—how he chose to defend, how he set up Ben's aggression, and most importantly, how he didn't step on or get stepped on by Ben's roaming right foot. As I watched Collin, I'd often find myself morphing into his mindset, mentally turning into the set-up partner, responsible for being the rock and not getting blown up by the young pro who was going to make it his priority to expose me.

For two months this became my obsession. I would've rather lost my senior pro matches than be the first dude to lose with Ben Johns. I went to the beach every morning and pushed myself through countless lateral, backward, and forward lunges in the soft sand. I would *not* be the senior pro to embarrass all the other senior pros.

At the US Open, when Ben and I walked on the court for our first-round match, I found myself almost hyperventilating. I had never felt as nervous in any athletic event I had competed in . . . ever. My heart was pounding, my hands were shaking, and I was breathing rapidly. Of course, I never showed Ben those nerves, but when our opponents made me hit the first third shot of the match and I put it in the bottom of the net, I think Ben knew and maybe even started laughing. I looked at him, smiled, and assured him I was fine.

I took a deep breath, tapped into my memory bank of the obsessive preparation I had grinded out for the past two months, and told myself that I was ready. After five nervous points, the countless hours of work I had put in started to reveal themselves. I let Ben dance around the court, as he does so well, but when it was my turn to battle, I made sure I did my job. Eventually settling in, I was able to execute the role I had visualized for two months and lean into the hours of intentional preparation to support Ben toward our US Open Split Age gold medal.

How we prepare for competition sets the stage for all that follows. The preparation leading up to a tournament—from mental and physical training to the tedium of packing a game bag—is not just ticking items off a readiness list. All the work I did before stepping on the court with Ben allowed me to be both physically prepared and mentally ready to find my stride amongst the most intense competitive stress I had ever felt. Cultivating the discipline to mentally and physically prepare before we pick up our paddles on game day is a mental toughness exercise itself. This chapter explores how to battle-ready our body and mind for tournament day and dives into: (1) how to make the most out of the weeks leading up to a tournament, (2) how to manage a good or bad day on the court, and (3) how to debrief after a tournament, no matter the result.

1. Pre-Tourney Preparation

A good rule of thumb is to ramp up your mental and physical preparation two weeks before your tournament. I can already hear some of y'all dismissing pre-tournament routines as a luxury of time only affordable by professional athletes. Let's debunk that fallacy. What I am proposing doesn't take any more time than you already spend on pickleball; it just redistributes the time you already spend.

Amateurs often allocate most, if not all, of their preparation time to playing rec games without dedicating any energy to preparing their minds for competition day. While getting on the court with your partner is important, it's only one piece of the pie. If I got to dictate how athletes distributed their time in the weeks preceding a tournament, I'd have them allot fifty percent of their pickleball hours to mental preparation. You read that right. I only want you physically on the court for half of your available time. While it is easier to mindlessly play rec, mentally preparing for the tournament day you want to unfold will uplevel your physical and mental game in ways that simply engaging in the physical grind could never accomplish.

Pre-Tournament: Mental Performance Preparation

Strategic Preparation: Scouting Reports

If you are familiar with any of the teams you'll be playing against at the tournament, consider creating scouting reports that evaluate your opponents' mental and physical strengths and weaknesses. First, if you are privy to your opponents' internal makeup, assess your opponents' mental toughness, triggers, and patience levels: Are they irritated by lobs, sun, wind, time-outs, or trash talk? Are they emboldened by certain mental tactics or physical styles of play? Do they lose patience quickly and want to end points prematurely? After assessing your opponents' mental blueprint, consider how they would assess and target *your* mental toughness, triggers, and patience level, then adjust your plan accordingly. Second, analyze each player's physical tendencies, including their playing style, dinking tendencies and wants, attacking tendences and wants, counter-attacking tendencies and wants, and dropping/driving tendencies and wants. Try filling out a rubric like this one:

Pre-Tournament Mental Performance Preparation

PLAYER SCOUTING REPORT	
Mental Toughness	*7/10*
Patience Level	*4/10*
Triggers	*Trash talking. Being hit at. Stare-downs. Opponents unfriendliness.*
Dinking Tendencies & Wants	*Dinks line when he gets pulled wide, so look to Erne often. Allows deep dinks to bounce, so be aggressive and power dink him to his feet.*
Attacking & Counter-Attacking Tendencies & Wants	*Only attacks off the bounce and mostly to the middle. When he attacks out of air, it's with BH and always to body straight ahead.*
Drop/Dive Tendencies & Wants	*Always slides right to hit two-handed BH. His body is weak and open.*
Playing Style	*Very slow and methodical. He'll only get aggressive when attacked.*

Finally, reflect on what you know about your competitors *as a team*. To craft a strategy for any given team, start by thinking about how your competitors like to play instinctively, regardless of their opponents. Next, try to predict how your opponents read *your* partnership's playing style and how they might adjust their play based on what they know about you. You can deepen your analysis by considering what your opponents did in the past when playing against you, whether it worked, and how you adjusted to them. The more you laser in on what your opponents *think about you*, the better plan you can put together.

A winning strategy isn't based on how *you want* to play as much as how *they don't want* you to play.

Remember, a winning strategy isn't based on how *you want* to play as much as how *they don't want* you to play.

Pre-Tournament Mental Performance

TEAM SCOUTING REPORT	
How does this team instinctively like to play?	*They want to work the point slowly and dare us to attack early. They love countering and are counting on us to lose patience and attack first. When we attack, we must be very intentional as to where and when.*
How do we need to adjust to this team based on what we know about their styles and patterns?	*If we play too fast, they earn points. Simultaneously, we can't play passively and fall into their game style. They're good enough to take advantage of our impatience, but we still need to dictate the tempo and game style.*
How will they adjust to us based on what they know about our styles and patterns?	*They will intentionally try to slow us down, knowing we'd rather play fast. They will dink us middle, attempting to cut off our attacking angles.*
If we played against them before, what worked and what didn't? How did we adjust? How did they adjust?	*We won in the past because we dictated the tempo and made them play at our pace. We stayed patient, but still played aggressively. They tried to slow us down by playing ultra slowly and methodically.*

The specificity of your game plan will depend on your partnership's makeup. For some, the more detailed information, the better. For others, too much information creates a mental traffic jam. Depending on the mental and physical skills in your partnership's arsenal, your game plan might simply be stylistic (aggressive/attack first or dink/reset/grind), or it might be more granular and include specifics like who/how/where to return, attack, and avoid.

Because no plan survives the impact of the battle, on game day you've got to be ready to pivot. If your preliminary plan isn't working, how will you adjust? While you can't perfectly predict what will happen, it's worth talking through potential adjustments ahead of time. It's the mental toughness equivalent of a deposit in a rainy-day fund; if you are ready for anything, you'll still be solvent if you have to make a few unexpected withdrawals.

Even with the best preparation, you still need to be able to make real-time strategic assessments and adjustments. After all, many amateurs won't know a single team in their bracket and need to create their entire game plan on the fly. Developing real-time strategic chops is a skill like any other that requires intentional practice and repetition. The lack of attention to building strategic savvy prematurely caps too many amateurs' progression. If you can't identify the strengths and vulnerabilities on *both sides* of the net, you will hit a ceiling far before your technical skills would merit.

To build this skill, make flexing your vision muscles as important as drilling your shots. As you reach the two-week window, every time you're on the court—drilling or playing a rec game—interrogate each point: Keep asking yourself, "Why does she keep hitting (X) shot, to (X) spot, in (X) situation? What does she think about our game that makes her want to design (X) game plan against us?" Lean into *their* mindset and watch what happens to *your own*. I know . . . that you know . . . that I know . . . that you know. With daily intentional focus, your sense of why your opponents are

> **Lean into their mindset and watch what happens to your own.**

doing what they're doing and what they believe about your patterns will quickly become more heightened.

Film Study & Visualization

Beyond learning to see the patterns unfolding in your own games, in the weeks leading up to a tournament, I'm a strong believer in the benefit of film study. Before you start mindlessly watching whatever tournament happens to be streaming, let's talk about what it means to watch pickleball as a *training exercise*. Film study for the purpose of improving our own game is an entirely different beast than watching a match for entertainment purposes. Rather than following the progression of the match, laser your focus on one player whose style of play resonates with you. For example, when Jill asked me to help pick a player for her to study, I narrowed the pool down to female players who use their length and strength offensively. It wouldn't make any sense for Jill, who is tall, strong, and tends toward a more aggressive playing style, to emulate a petite player or one with a more patient, grinding style.

Once you've identified a player, pull up some film, put your body on top of her body, and sync up with the way she moves on the court. Rather than trying to take in her whole style of play, choose *one or two aspects of her game* to observe, envision, and emulate. While you're watching, pause the video, and visualize what you just watched play out with you and your partner. The more you can drop into the player, blur out the back and forth of the match, and actively visualize yourself executing what you see, the more you will be able to incorporate your film study into your own game.

Finally, as tournament day approaches, commit to finding quiet moments each day to visualize executing the successful patterns, counters, and adjustments you've discerned from being an intentional observer of your games and those of the pros you've chosen to study. Even though it's easier to turn the brain off and mindlessly play, quieting the mind and body to engage in a visualization practice *is* a game-changer.

Pre-Tournament: Physical Preparation

Use your time on the court wisely: Distribute your court hours between purposeful drilling to clean up vulnerabilities and rec games with your partner to iron out any kinks in your partnership. Avoid practicing with your tournament opponents unless you want to hand out free information on how to get better at playing against you. If you wouldn't show your cards while playing poker, then don't trot out your strengths and vulnerabilities to your opponents right before game day. Finally, the day before the tournament, choose your practice opponents carefully to provide the mental and physical opportunities that will best prepare you for the day to come.

How to Prepare for a Tournament

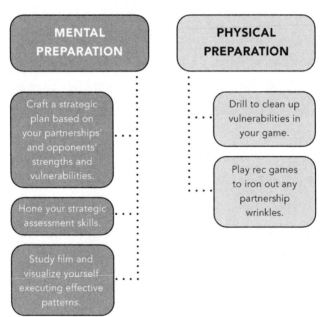

MENTAL PREPARATION

PHYSICAL PREPARATION

Craft a strategic plan based on your partnerships' and opponents' strengths and vulnerabilities.

Drill to clean up vulnerabilities in your game.

Hone your strategic assessment skills.

Play rec games to iron out any partnership wrinkles.

Study film and visualize yourself executing effective patterns.

2. Tournament Day

Tournament Day Rituals

I'm a big proponent of developing a set of pregame rituals for tournament day. The morning of the tournament, you should be able to automatically cycle through the essential tasks required to prepare your mind and body without having to allocate any bandwidth to the contents of the process. Methodically following a preordained routine before stepping on the court helps to "flip the switch" and instinctively lock into tournament mode. Consistently executing a routine in the hours leading up to go-time also helps calm pregame jitters and sets you up to confidently manage the day ahead.

Benefits of Pre-Tourney Rituals

> **1.** Makes pre-tourney routines easy and effortless

> **2.** Creates a "mental flip switch" that helps drop you into tourney-mode

> **3.** Helps calm pre-game jitters

> **4.** Gives a confidence boost

Everyone's routines will be different but should cover the basics of mental preparation (visualization) and physical readiness (nutrition, hydration, dynamic stretching, rolling, and warm-up).

Pre-Tourney Ritual Checklist

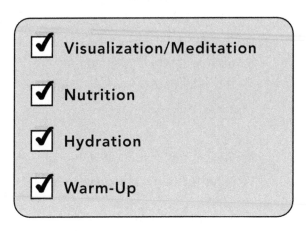

Information Gathering

Once you reach the venue, it's open season for information gathering. Your opponents will be streaming free information about themselves from the moment they arrive at the courts. **From warming up until the last match is played, look for clues on and off the court about your opponents' strengths and vulnerabilities:**

- How do your opponents respond after a miss? Do they show a subtle yet noticeable drop in confidence?

- How do they react to each other's mistakes? Do they disconnect or fight it out as a team?
- Are they upset about an opponent's strategy? Are they grumpy about the referee, sun, or wind?

Every bit of information has value and should be stored away for the perfect moment to monopolize on the intel you've gathered about your opponents' internal makeup that day.

If your opponents are savvy, they will be watching you and your partner too. Throughout the day, if you're tired, discouraged, mad, or annoyed with your partner or anything else, that's normal; tournaments are stressful. Now isn't the time to show it. Get your poker face on, stay positive, and keep your head up. Never give your opponents a free supply of confidence; make them *earn* it.

What to Do When You're Winning

In pickleball, getting to 10-X is no guarantee you'll cinch the win, no matter your opponents' score. Finishing is a mental performance skill that can trip up even professionals, so it's worth giving thought to the mindset and strategies that will help get you across the finish line.

Let's assume you've battled your way to 10-9 and it's your serve. In these close matches when victory is spitting distance away, many players falter and allow their opponents to fight their way back to the win. While the details of how to finish will depend on the specifics of the match up, the winning strategy is virtually always the same: **Keep doing what you did to get there. If you've been attacking, keep attacking. If you've grinded your opponents down with slow, muddy, 700-ball dink rallies, keep grinding.**

Often players are tempted to switch things up in the final stretch to keep their opponents off balance and guessing. All too often, when a team should be slamming the door shut on their opponents, they go into survival mode and begin to play "not to lose." Instead of keeping their foot on the gas and forcing the other side to make a strategic adjustment, they adjust away from the winning strategy and create an opening for their opponents to come back for the win. Once you're at 10-x, the most effective closing strategy is to continue doing what you did to get you to game point in the first place. Call a time-out if need be, and get on the same page with your partner. Ask one another what got you to this point, and commit to continue driving home that strategy. **If your opponents make a comeback, it's okay to pivot, but only if they prove your game plan is no longer working. Otherwise, confidently keep implementing the strategy that got you there.**

What to Do When You're Winning

☑ Confidently keep implementing the strategy that put you ahead.

☑ Stay aggressive and keep playing "to win."

☑ Only pivot from your winning strategy if your opponents make a comeback and prove your game plan is no longer working.

Finally, beyond strategy, the ability to close out games is a learned mindset skill predicated on exposure. We can't drill it into existence, so the only way we get better at it is by exposing ourselves to the make-or-break moments over and over again. The more often we negotiate the stress of match point, the easier it will become to effectively manage it, keep the fear at bay, and remain aggressive and strategically intentional.

What to Do When You're Losing

How to fight your way back when the game isn't going your way will depend on the specifics of the match. Regardless of the strategic details, we can all get on the same mental page. Often when amateurs are behind, they lose patience, get desperate, and try to hit knock-out punches to get all the points back at once. Instead, **if you are down, tunnel your focus onto the present point and ask yourself, "What is our singular intention? How can we win *this next point* right here?"**

Tying your intention to the point in front of you rather than focusing on erasing your opponents' lead has been preached by coaches for years. Yet as often repeated as the advice is, it's incredibly difficult to do. In the emotional, fearful moments, our minds race, our fight response triggers, and we instinctively rush, thinking we need to hasten the comeback process. Being in the hole is uncomfortable, so we intuitively want to make our way out as quickly as possible. If we are rushing our comeback, we won't be able to slow down enough to see and make the necessary strategic adjustments.

> **If we are rushing our comeback, we won't be able to slow down enough to see and make the necessary strategic adjustments.**

We need to trick our bodies into doing the opposite of what our minds are telling us to do. To short-circuit the impulse to keep blindly rushing forward, slow down your walk after a point, lengthen your breath, and take more time in between points. If you can slow down your body, you'll have a better shot of becoming more intentional in your actions. **The next time you're down, take a time-out, go into slow-motion mode, and choose *one* singular intention with your partner.** Getting your wheels to stop spinning obviously doesn't guarantee you'll win, but it will improve your clarity of mind and give you the best chance for a comeback.

What to Do When You're Losing

- ✓ Don't rush to close the gap in the score.

- ✓ Focus on the present point.

- ✓ Slow down your walk & lengthen your breath.

- ✓ Take a time out.

- ✓ Choose one intention with your partner.

Peripheral Mastery: Head-Down, Eyes-Locked

Pickleball ain't tennis, and the tournament environment is as different as the sport. If you're expecting

Wimbledon etiquette, buckle up and get ready. Pickleball tournaments can feel like the Wild West, even during professional matches: balls rolling on the court, music blaring, players walking through your court, competitors bickering with the referee a court away, spectators talking loudly. Getting frustrated by the chaos won't stop it, so part of your job is to learn to manage it.

A technique I learned from one of my tennis coaches, Head-Down, Eyes-Locked, is an effective way to block out distractions and stay focused on the next point. With so many opportunities to be distracted, it's imperative to take control of our minds. Head-Down, Eyes-Locked is exactly what it sounds like: our head is pointed down and our eyes are locked onto the ground as we walk or are waiting for the next point to start. Why? This ensures that our eyes (and consequently our minds) don't stray to the distractions in front of us. The moment our eyes focus on the player running through our court, the spectator yelling at his friend, or the guy arguing with the referee, we instantly lose connection to our blueprint. We then have to take time to redirect our attention back to the next point. How many times have we lost focus for a second and then missed the next return or serve?

By keeping our head down and eyes locked on the ground in between points, we can develop "peripheral mastery," the ability to keep everything in our peripheral vision blurry. Nothing outside our focused eyesight is clear, and the sounds around us are just white noise. When I'm in this focused mode, I have no idea who is watching the match and can't hear a word from anyone outside my partner and the referee. This level of focus is attainable by all players, regardless of age or level, but the practice starts with what we do in between points when distractions are screaming at us to lose focus.

Tournament Day Tips Summary

INFORMATION GATHERING

Observe your opponents throughout the day to learn about their strengths, vulnerabilities, and mindset.

WHEN YOU'RE WINNING

To close out a win, unless your opponents prove your game plan is no longer working, keep doing what you did to take the lead.

WHEN YOU'RE LOSING

Resist the temptation to hasten a comeback. Slow down your body and mind and choose one singular intention for each point ahead of you.

PERIPHERAL MASTERY

To block out distractions, make everything in your peripheral vision blurry, lasering your focus on the point ahead of you. Between points, keep your head down and eyes locked on the ground in front of you.

3. Post-Tournament Debrief: Making the Most Out of a Win or Loss

Now that your tournament day is over, it's time to either give yourself a high five or dust yourself off and regroup. After a tournament, take a day or two off to reset, mentally even more than physically. Tournament play takes an incredible amount of physical and mental energy. Even if you typically eat, sleep, and breathe pickleball, give your body and mind the chance to shut it down completely before getting back out there.

If things didn't go your way, take your day off and then get back to training. It's fine to be mad, but don't let that energy go to waste. Use it to fuel the work you need to do to achieve a better result next time.

If you filmed your matches, watch them and mine them for data to drive your training. Even if it wasn't your day and watching the film is as tempting as poking your eyeballs, it's mandatory if you want to get better. If you don't have the benefit of video, after a few days have passed, take notes on what you think happened. What worked? What didn't work? Where were you vulnerable? What were your strengths? Use your observations to answer the question that all tournaments beg: "Now what?" Even though it's important to identify your vulnerabilities, it is as important to recognize your strengths. Too many players go down a negative rabbit hole and eventually blind themselves to their superpowers. When you review your tournament, consider it obligatory to identify the things you did well as well as the areas of your game that require more attention.

While you have your notebook out, jot down your recollections of the players that you came across. Most likely, you'll meet up with them again, so memorialize the information you learned while your memory is fresh.

POST-TOURNAMENT DEBRIEF
1.   What worked and what didn't work?
2.   What were our strengths?
3.   What were our vulnerabilities?
4.   Now what? How do our post-tourney observations influence our training?
5.   What did we learn about our opponents' strengths and vulnerabilites?

Finally, once all the work is done, I think the best thing you can do is break your clean eating and enjoy a donut. At least that's what I do.

JILL

You may have divined by now that I'm not what you'd call footloose and fancy free. I love checklists, organizational systems, spreadsheets, plans, contingency plans, and all the mind-numbingly boring accouterments of your favorite Type-A friends. There are two exceptions to my fastidious ways: driving and tournament preparation. The most unexpectedly laid back driver you've ever met, I enjoy the scenery, spend all my time in the slow lane, and am often lost on the same roads I've traveled for twenty years as I blissfully poke along. If that surprises you, just wait until you hear how laissez-faire I am when it comes to tournament preparation. If you're the type of person who learns from another person's mistakes, omissions, and oversights, I am your gal because I've made them all. To my credit, I have never forgotten to wear shoes to a tournament, which is more than my teenage sons can say about many days of their lives.

Typically, I write about putting Dayne's suggestions into practice. Implementing Dayne's higher-level tournament preparation from the outset would have been like asking me to defend a doctoral dissertation when I was mastering shoe tying. If you're reading this book, you probably don't need the Tournament Preparation for Dummies guide, but I did! For the other five people who stepped out of line while tournament smarts were being handed out, let me tell you some of the basics I've learned the hard way.

1. Read the Rules

I wish I had a good excuse for showing up to multiple tournaments without reading the rules. I suspect I was forced to review the Federal Rules of Civil Procedure one too many times and have unconsciously boycotted all future rule reading. While Dayne probably didn't mention reading the rules because he assumed everyone would know to do that, I know I am not the only one because I am *that person* who everyone asks for help. My resting-smile face draws confused people to me like a moth to a flame. Of course, asking me about the tournament rules was a serious miscalculation, but I'm honored to look competent or at least approachable.

It turns out that the rules include important information that will shape your day. Often amateur games aren't refereed, so if no one knows a rule, you either have to chase down the tournament director or engage in tense, uninformed discussions with your opponents. From personal experience, I recommend neither. Besides, walking in blind adds unnecessary uncertainty to a day already filled with more than enough of it, so be a reasonable human and read them.

2. Don't Make Big Changes to Your Game Right Before a Tournament

I've tried out last-minute changes to just about every aspect of my game. Spoiler alert: it never works out well. I'll never forget the look on Dayne's face when my partner told him that I unwrapped and played with a new paddle—a model I had never used before—at a tournament. "You did what?"

Typically, he can find something positive to say about some of the crazy choices I make, but that one left him speechless. Suffice it to say, unless your only other choice is to play with your bare hand, I'd advise against last-minute equipment changes.

Unless you really want to take your partner by surprise with unparalleled inconsistency, I'd also recommend a hard pass on changing up how you execute your fundamentals right before a tournament. In my early days of pickleball, before I was working with Dayne, my friends and I took two lessons from different instructors with very different teaching styles a couple of days before a tournament. In those two ill-fated lessons, each instructor taught us a different approach to getting to the kitchen. In the first lesson, the instructor was begging us to slow down and take our time. In the next lesson, the instructor urged us to crash the net. Of course, both were right, depending on the circumstances, but we were a bit too green to be able to discern what to do when, especially since we had only given ourselves forty-eight hours to figure it out before our tournament. On the upside, at the tournament, our own confusion created so much pandemonium that we also successfully confused the pants off our opponents and somehow scraped our way to the podium. The thought bubbles of the more composed teams that we beat shouted what we all were thinking, "How did those clowns pull that off?"

Most people aren't taking lessons from two different instructors right before a tournament, but in my experience, at the 3.0 to 4.0 level, even one lesson too close to competition day has its risks. I can always feel the wheels turning when I am fresh off a lesson and trying to incorporate a new strategy or skill. In this early stage of learning, my mind is too busy to be able to drop into a rhythm on the court. I suspect the same admonition likely wouldn't apply to more experienced players with deeper knowledge of the game and more robust fundamentals. For greener players, consider hedging your bets and leaning into what you know rather than cluttering your mind with new intel.

3. Pay Attention to Hydration and Nutrition

As someone who came from endurance sports, pickleball seemed so mild in its athletic demands that I completely ignored hydration and caloric needs. I paid for my nonchalant attitude more than once. During tournaments, my focus is pulled in so many directions that I often forget to properly eat and hydrate. Since I've learned I can't trust my hunger and thirst instincts, I now treat myself like a toddler and have put myself on a compulsory drink and snack schedule throughout the day.

In addition to serious health risks that come with dehydration, from a purely mental performance perspective, I've watched my mental capacity, and that of my partner, nosedive if we let our tanks run too close to empty. My guess is that this skill comes more naturally to most, but as the only mom on this writing staff, this is your friendly reminder to pack lots of good snacks and drinks and then gobble them up. See how much easier my suggestions are to implement than Dayne's big ideas?

4. Try It All Out and Then Do What Works for You

Pre-Tournament Preparation: Less Is More

Having recently mastered tournament skills for the absentminded, by the time this chapter rolled around, I'd just started to feel ready to incorporate some of Dayne's higher-level preparation strategies.

When Dayne told me I should spend half of my preparation time on mental preparation, however, I was dubious and not subtle about my reservations: "You're telling *me* that I should only spend fifty percent of my time on the court even though I don't have the touch or racquet sport experience you have?" Ever the chess player with way too much free intel on how to bait his opponent, Dayne casually replied, "Yes, but I'm hesitant to even suggest it because most people won't have the discipline to do it." Insert eyeroll here.

I tried. I really did. While writing this chapter, I slugged my way through film study, visualization, scouting reports, strategic planning, and more film study. I learned two important lessons about myself: First, thinking more about pickleball off the court risks turning up the mental noise I have to reckon with on the court. Perhaps because I am naturally such a chronic overthinker, dedicating too much headspace to pickleball landed me more in my mind on the court and less in my body. If I've learned anything through pickleball, the quieter my mind, the more able my body. I suspect that's why I am so cavalier about all the pre-tourney prep details. Not giving too much attention to the tournament ahead of time helps me manage my pregame jitters in the way that methodically preparing helps Dayne manage his.

Second, as I fought to stay awake through film study and visualization practice, I realized that allotting half of my time to mental preparation isn't a ratio that appeals to me given my personal goals. The more pickleball I've played, the clearer it has become that my goals aren't linked to reaching any given podium or ranking. I'd like to get better at showing up on the court as a more supportive partner and a better version of myself; for me, that often means turning the intensity volume knob down rather than up.

I love the grind of improvement; however, equally, if not more important, is the joy pickleball brings me. With kids, work, and the need to sleep, I can't grow the number of hours I dedicate to the game, and I'm not willing to reduce my time on the court. Trying to carve out the time to study film and schedule a dedicated visualization practice made pickleball start to feel like a job. The more pickleball felt like "work," the less I enjoyed myself on the court, and the worse I played. Dayne said it best when he recently told me, "The medals come for you when you go out to have fun with your partner." For the one millionth time during this process, I'm in awe of the mental fortitude it takes to play a sport professionally and am so grateful that I get to just be a goofball on the court.

Tournament Day Tips: Work in Progress

While Dayne's *pre*-tournament preparation strategies didn't serve me as well as they would many, his tournament *day* strategies helped me with some mental housekeeping I hadn't even realized needed to be done.

What to Do When Winning and Losing

You know how when you learn a new word, you start to hear it all the time and think, *How did I get this far in life without knowing that word?* As soon as Dayne and I talked about how to close a game, I wondered how I had ever gotten to eleven since previously getting to ten brought out the crazy in me.

In close matches, I tended to swing between two extremes once we got to ten. Either I'd become passive as Dayne predicted, or I'd become reckless to end the tension as quickly as possible by rashly speeding up the play. Somehow in the heat of the battle, staying the winning course never dawned on me. I love when Dayne's advice doesn't require hours of visualizing and still works. This has been one of those gems!

When trying to reverse a downhill trajectory, I also previously would default to ping-ponging between impulsive aggression and passivity. (Is anyone else sensing a pattern here?) Finding the sweet spot of slowing-down-the-body and quieting-the-mind enough to make good choices without petering out altogether has been a tough balancing act for me. Dayne's competitive drive runs like a firehose compared to my California drought-compliant sink faucet, so sometimes I wonder whether he has more range to play with when he slows himself down. In yoga, we practice these slowing-down skills all the time, but they aren't followed by trying to crush our competitors' dreams. At first when I slowed down, I'd lose my intensity to the point of lackadaisy. With practice, I've come closer to finding the calm intensity, or what one of my partners calls "calm goodness," that allows me to systematically fight for one point at a time.

Maintaining Focus Among Chaos

Should anyone doubt whether Dayne implements the strategies he recommends, I can offer eyewitness testimony that he has conquered "peripheral mastery," or he really likes to pretend he doesn't know me. Well into writing this book, I played at a tournament in which Dayne was also competing. Because of close quarters between courts, Dayne and I ended up standing shoulder to shoulder and directly across from one another multiple times. The man even knocked into me once. Since he said nothing, I said nothing, figuring he needed space. At the end of the tournament, I texted him about having fun watching in person, to which he responded, "You were at the tournament???"

If Dayne occupies one extreme of peripheral mastery, I sit at the other end of the spectrum. Until recently, when Dayne trained all the fun out of me, I chitchatted, looked around, and took it all in. Now that he's made me into a pickleball robot, I, too, will appear aloof and unfriendly, even to my own octogenarian mother. Okay, so that's not true, but I have tried to reign it in at least on the court. Keeping my eyes down between points has helped filter out visual distractions, but it almost amplifies my startle response to sudden noises. I am hoping that eventually the benefit of peripheral visual mastery will percolate down to my sensitive ears. Until then, if you're not sure if it's me at a tournament, just clap your hands loudly. If I jump out of my skin, you'll know you've found me.

Having go-to strategies for what to do on the court no matter what is happening reminds me of what appealed to me about law school: the availability of an orderly set of "if > then" statements to follow regardless of the underlying facts you encounter. As someone who likes to have a Plan A, B, C, D, E, and F, knowing that I have several mental strategies to draw upon has helped me get out of my mind and into my body, which seems to know a lot more than my mind, at least on the court.

Post-Tournament Debrief

Left to my own devices, post-tournament, my mind often falls into old habits of fixating exclusively on what went wrong and what I could have done better. Once, after winning gold, my partner and I spent our entire two-hour car ride home dissecting what we could have done better, almost willfully refusing to acknowledge that we must have done something right to get us to the top of the podium.

Working with Dayne put a hard stop to my negatively biased post-tournament analysis. He put me on the short leash I so clearly needed: No longer am I allowed to let my mind go on an undisciplined free fall into my perceived shortcomings;

I also have to identify what I did well. That more balanced assessment better informs the purpose of any post-tournament analysis: Answering the question, *Now what? How do I train now to fortify my vulnerabilities and amplify my strengths?*

Even with practice, I can still sometimes get lost in post-tourney fun house mirrors where mistakes take on grotesque proportions and good moments all but disappear. Following Dayne's ground rules of waiting a day or two after a disappointing loss and *requiring* myself to undertake a fair-minded evaluation has helped. Knowing that I'll have to report my findings back to Dayne, who has no patience for my dives into the "I suck" deep end, also holds my feet to the fire. Because the purpose of working with Dayne is moving beyond needing his hand-holding, I've started transitioning my post-tourney analysis from Dayne to my partners, trusting that between the two of us, we can come up with a complete picture of where we shined and where we need to grow.

Here's what I am most proud of: I *have* started to be able to see what I do well sooner with less screw-turning. The best news is that my gains have happened in the arena that matters most to me: my mental performance. I do a better job of staying connected with my partners through wins and losses. I bounce back from head-spinning losses faster. Sometimes I even have enough discipline to follow a game plan! Most importantly, even during the chaos of a tournament, I've begun to reconnect with the joy that brought me to the court in the first place.

---

1. The split age event teams up one pro player with one senior pro player.

CONCLUSION

Where to Go from Here

DAYNE

NOW THAT YOU'VE FINISHED the book, hopefully you
feel inspired to put in *more* or at least *different* work
toward your game. With so much information, where
do you begin? Mental performance training isn't
susceptible to a one-size-fits-all sequential path
that will yield predictably paced and measurable
improvements. Just like you'll benefit the most from
drilling that is tailored to your specific on-court
assets and liabilities, your unique mental strengths

and vulnerabilities should inform your mindset training.

While the mental performance strategies that work best will be different for everyone, the qualities and mindset required to navigate the treacherous waters of mental game training are universal. No matter who you are, from the top athlete in your field to a novice competitor, the process of optimizing mental performance demands untold patience and tolerance for discomfort, setbacks, and uncertainty. Rather than worrying too much about *where* to start, get intentional about the mindset you'll bring to the process and the tools and support systems you'll draw upon when you hit roadblocks.

I'd recommend starting by setting your expectations for how the process will look and feel. Shifting habitual thought patterns and fortifying our mindset demands an unimaginable amount of waiting: Drill, wait. Rec, wait. Tournament, wait. Rinse and repeat for weeks, months, years. It is incredibly easy to get ensnared by the fast trap that tricks us into believing that results should follow at the same pace we've come to expect in other areas of our fast-paced lives. Mindset training, however, isn't susceptible to the rate of return we're accustomed to in our world of instantaneous gratification. The concepts we've talked about aren't meant to be mastered today, this week, or this month; they are strategies to incorporate and practice over a lifetime.

At times, it may even feel like the more work you're putting in, the further you find yourself drifting from your goals. This frustrating incubation period is ultimately what breaks players or pushes them beyond their peers. The best athletes embrace and invite the waiting game because they know their resolve won't falter as their competition slowly falls away. Gutting out the physical grind is not the differentiator; waiting for the hours of practice to align with physical and mental execution is what separates the good athletes from the great. Just like mentally preparing for a tournament with innumerable uncontrollable elements, the best advice I can offer to level-up your mental game is to *pre-accept that progress unfolds on its own timeline.*

If your patience starts to flag, lock your eyes on the horizon and fight the temptation to ride the highs and lows of the micro ups and downs. If we took a microscope to our day-to-day results, we'd inevitably see massive fluctuation in our outcomes. The short term is filled with grind, struggle, wins, pain, losses, fatigue, celebrations, exhaustion, more losses, and more wins. No more should we get high on our own supply than we should let our tough days become the puppeteer of our self-belief. Decide that your long-term vision of yourself is your compass, not yesterday's wins or losses.

> Decide that your long-term vision of yourself is your compass, not yesterday's wins or losses.

In the moments when picking yourself up off the ground yet again feels like one time too many, ask for a hand up. While elevating your performance is work that can only be done by you, it doesn't need to be done alone. There isn't an athlete on this planet who doesn't need a lifeline at some point. Align yourself with a partner, friend, or coach who can help you see the forest again when you've gotten lost in the trees. Besides, if nothing else, sharing the ups and downs of the journey with someone is a lot more fulfilling.

Bringing this book to fruition tested my resolve and self-belief on multiple occasions. Over the last fifteen years, I attempted to write a version of this book more times than I can count. When I look back now at the times that I fumbled through half-written chapters, I realize I simply wasn't ready yet. I needed to mature as a person, coach, and athlete before I could commit my beliefs to the page. This book had to unfold on its own timeline too. If I had let the mounting short-term evidence that writing a book wasn't in the cards for me dictate my beliefs about what was possible, I wouldn't have agreed to the very off-the-cuff suggestion by Jill to write a book together.

There, of course, was another critical difference this time around. I didn't go it alone. Downloading the ideas from my mind to the page with Jill was a fundamentally different experience than my previous solo attempts. Coaching, more than playing, is what lights me up and makes my mind search for better or different ways to help athletes optimize their mental and physical performance. This book was essentially the longest, most closely documented coaching session of my career with an athlete whose question-asking was only matched by her dedication to the process. Finally, our accountability to one another kept us moving forward when it would have been easier to abandon this book at the same junkyard housing all the other half-written books.

As much as writing the book challenged my patience, it also tested my long-held coaching beliefs. Learning how to better clear the gray areas for Jill demanded that I refine how I communicated concepts and strategies that I had been coaching for years and made me more compassionate to the amateur player's experience.

Watching Jill evolve over the course of writing the book has been one of the most gratifying parts of the experience for me. Early in the writing process, Jill would often suggest that we pull her part of the book and make it into a more traditional coaching book told from only my perspective. Despite the many times I disagreed with her, she couldn't understand why her journey would have value to anyone but her. She also wasn't sure if she was comfortable sharing her inner demons for the world to critique. Without the benefit of having walked this path with countless athletes over the last thirty years, Jill couldn't always see that her fears, vulnerabilities, and doubts were universal.

It's easy to conclude that we're alone in our battles with self-belief, but the opposite couldn't be truer: it is the quintessential human experience. The more she wrote, the more she stripped away the protective shield that she had worn to hide what she once thought was weakness and let her vulnerabilities sit unmasked on the page.

Beyond her growing confidence, the biggest change I saw in Jill came from the constant game of tug-of-war playing out between the aggressive athlete who lived on one shoulder and the kind and sensitive person firmly rooted on the other. Early on, she seemed to believe she had to choose one over the other, or at a minimum, couldn't be successful while leaving both intact. It's a tightrope she is still learning to walk, but through her successes and failures, I've watched her increasingly connect her fierce, athletic self with the compassionate woman everyone knows her to be.

JILL

Remember when you were young and thought that once you were an adult, you'd have it all figured out? Maybe you imagined as I did that the tincture of time and the very process of growing up would miraculously make you wise? Then suddenly you find yourself at the age you previously identified as "old enough to know" and instead of having all the answers, you realize how much there is left to learn. That's a lot of what writing this book felt like.

When Dayne started to coach me, I was under the illusion that a couple of mental nips and tucks would plug all my mental leaks on the court. I thought that learning how to think differently on the court would be a finite process with incremental, attainable steps that I could check off as I went. Like building a house, I assumed I'd methodically complete each phase—from pouring the foundation to erecting the frame to shingling the roof—and then I'd have crafted the perfectly constructed house to enjoy forever. It turns out that transforming your mindset is less like a project with a start, middle, and end, and more like peeling back the scales of an infinitely layered onion: Unwinding one mental habit and replacing it with a new way of thinking only seemed to reveal the next strata of work that needed to be done.

The process was much harder than I thought it would be and feels far from over. I can't say that Dayne didn't warn me. His belief in my abilities on and off the court always outpaced my own but also frequently came with ominous warnings about the discomfort, pain, and disappointment that I'd have to endure to reach the level he believed I could. Dayne often concluded a positive prognostication about my future with, "That is . . . if you don't quit first." While I would nod at him, in my mind, I was thinking, *Boy, does this guy have a flair for the dramatic.*

What could possibly drive me to quit a sport that I loved so much? While I certainly knew women on the 5.0 or bust train, I never was attached to reaching a specific goal, so what did I have to lose? Given how dismissive I had been of his admonitions, it came as a complete shock that over the course of writing this book, I did, in fact, consider retiring my pickleball paddle more than once.

As Dayne already intimated, one of the most challenging parts of last year has been figuring out how to negotiate the two dueling parts of my nature: my sensitive, empathic side with my intensely focused competitive side. Pickleball wasn't my first rodeo trying to balance the two. I felt similarly conflicted as a litigator: On the one hand, applying every ounce of myself to fiercely advocating for my client. On the other hand, feeling the weight of the discontent so often borne by all parties to litigation. And we all know how that ended—with me leaving the law. That, of course, is a massive simplification of why I stopped practicing law, but the similarity of the internal conflict I felt in my legal practice and on the court isn't lost on me.

We so rarely are afforded do-overs in life, but pickleball offered me a second shot to more successfully negotiate the two. Dayne never believed that I needed to forsake one part of myself for the other and reframed my unlikely combination of attributes as a superpower. Rather than lobotomizing some of my best parts, he helped me craft a mental toggle switch that lets me alternatively draw upon or quiet the different parts of me that serve important purposes on and off the court. The switch is made up of a dash of pre-acceptance, a smidge of visualization, more than a cup of unconditional confidence, and a metric ton of remaining committed to my internal goals over any external measure of success. The switch is still sticky and fails me at times, but so long as I can remember to look at the long-term arc of my progress, I can see that the needle is moving in the right direction both in my pickleball and personal worlds.

Finally, as became glaringly obvious throughout this process, reckoning with the many heads of my perfectionistic tendencies tested my patience for change on more than one occasion. Perhaps the greatest irony of writing this book is that the attention it drew to me became one of my bigger hurdles to feeling more confident on the court. Once Dayne started to publicly post about the book, I felt an acute, albeit self-imposed pressure to have already mastered my own mindset. In my head, since I had access to the best coach and was writing a book about mental performance, then I "should" no longer struggle with my mental game. With all my efforts to let go of my perfectionism through pickleball, I had created a new unrealistic standard to which to hold myself. Before I could see the trap I had set for myself, the increasing pressure I put on myself manifested in a nasty, embarrassing case of the "service yips" that temporarily killed my love of the game. During the months that I couldn't serve a ball into the very large square across from me, quitting crossed my mind more than once. For everything Dayne had taught me, it was in those really tough moments that he shined. His belief in me and ability to see that I was experiencing a normal, temporary performance blip resuscitated me many times.

I don't know that many athletes struggle with the issues that can get me wrapped around the axle and that made me question the relevance of including so much of my personal experience in the book. After multiple showdowns with Dayne about pressing "control all + delete" on my sections of the book, he not only wore me down but also convinced me that I was missing the point. The value of sharing my experience has nothing to do with whether anyone else's mental hiccups bear resemblance to mine. Rather, we all have our own variety of them, even if we don't talk much about them with one another. The most powerful support Dayne gave me over our year together was normalizing both the ways that I struggled and how challenging I found it to deactivate my mental tripwires.

My hope is that being honest about my two-steps forward/one-step back path helps do for you what Dayne was able to do for me. Perhaps it makes you feel less irredeemable on the days that you can only see how far you have left to go rather than how far you've come. To the extent you, too, thought Dayne was being hyperbolic when he warned you about the patience required to elevate your performance, I've already had to eat crow on that one, so my two cents are that you take his word for it. Finally, while working to build mental resilience on and off the court is harder than I ever imagined, if my experience is predictive, the grind is more than worth the reward, especially when you get to share the ride.

ABOUT THE AUTHORS

Dayne Gingrich is a mental performance and pickle-ball coach to professional and amateur players and the top men's Senior Pro pickleball player in the world. He brings his lifelong study of mindset training to optimize performance on and off the pickleball court.

⬡ @dayne_gingrich   ⬛ @DayneGingrich

Jill Martin is an attorney turned personal trainer, yoga teacher, and pickleball fanatic. Having filed her last legal brief, she now uses her knowledge of the body and passion for all things pickleball to help amateur and professional players keep injuries at bay and move better on the court.

⬡ @PickleballYogi   ⬛ @PickleballYogi

Printed in Great Britain
by Amazon